JOB <u>*MEETS*</u> *ELIHU*

Job's Mediator and Answer to Prayer

Eli M. Borden, PhD

JOB ^{Meets} ELIHU

Printed by CreateSpace, North Charleston, SC.
https://www.createspace.com/3944092

Dedication

This book is dedicated to my wife Wilsie and our growing family.

Children:

Eddie & Roxy Borden, David & Tammy Lunday, David & Cheri Ferneding, Sonya Richardson, Steve & Valorie Ruth, J.W. & Lori Richardson

Grandchildren:

Elyssa Borden, Ethan Lunday, Makayla Lunday, Tyler Ferneding, Hunter Ferneding, Ashleigh Ferneding, Derek Morrow, Greg & Candice Hammond, Matthew Ruth, Nathan & Elena Ruth, Benjamin & Katie Ruth, Samuel Ruth, Abigail Wilsie Ruth, Caleb Richardson, Skyler Richardson, Bethany Richardson, Chloe Richardson

Great Grandchildren:

Truman Hammond, Julian Hammond, Gabriel Ruth, Trinity Ruth, Ethan Ruth, Ellie Ruth, Evan Ruth, Natalie Ruth, Anthony Ruth

Special Thanks:

This author is deeply indebted to many people who have been instrumental in the creation of this book. After realizing the importance of Elihu in the book of *Job*, I have presented many lessons and have had many discussions with Christians across the nation. I would love to name all who helped in the process, but I know I would miss some.

However, special thanks to Donnie and Margaret Rogers for their consistent reminders to get the job done, and a thanks for their reading and comments on the manuscript before finalization.

Thanks also to my sister Fran Borden and step-daughter Sonya Richardson for helping edit the material, and a special thanks to my wife and soul-mate Wilsie for the cover design and for formatting the manuscript into book form.

None of this could have taken place without God's answer to many prayers for insights and direction in understanding and explaining the book of *Job*. Many times I have awakened in the middle of the night with better ways to explain the deep concepts within the book. I have often been aware of the LORD's presence. Thanks to God for the marvelous book of *Job* and for answering prayers for insight and guidance in putting this volume together.

Synopsis of *Job*

Job, a righteous, prosperous, and arrogant man, is devastated after losing his wealth and health almost overnight. His three friends try to help him through his ordeal, but their ineptness leads to Job's increasing anger directed at them and at God. The debate continues to deteriorate as his friends are unable to calm Job, but a puzzling character named Elihu enters the fray with shocking credentials and fresh insights that silence Job and his friends. Elihu prepares the way for Job's meeting with the Almighty, and circumstances are reversed once Job humbles himself.

Preface

– REASONS FOR STUDYING THE SUFFERING OF JOB

Have you ever found yourself in the middle of an "alligator pond" and wondered, "Why me"? There are no easy answers to the question; however, a proper comprehension of the book of *Job* will go a long way in better understanding the purpose and role of suffering. Better yet, this Bible story also gives answers for surviving life's tragedies and coming out on the other side in better condition than before. *Job* is the only book of the Bible to refer or describe an alligator, called Leviathan, which I will later show to also be a symbol of Satan. Job certainly faced his "alligator pond" and showed us the way to overcome adverse situations.

The worst "alligator pond" I have ever faced began in 1977 when my first wife Marian began having episodes and symptoms later diagnosed as Multiple Sclerosis. The announcement was difficult to take, but the alligators would get much larger because MS is a debilitating disease. We later learned that only 1 in 1,000 who suffer with MS have the progressive form Marian was experiencing. Steadily losing ground, she became a total invalid in 1982, the same year my dad was diagnosed with cancer. All three of my children were in school, so we shared responsibilities in meeting needs that grew each month.

Beginning in the summer of 1982 I had many things rip at my health. First I had to go through knee surgery following a collision in church league softball. Shortly after getting the cast removed from my right leg, I broke my left leg in a car accident. To complicate things even further, I developed a painful kidney stone.

One late afternoon a well-meaning friend came to visit me. When I opened the door, he said, "I came to hear your confession; you have done something to displease the Lord, or all this would not be happening." My immediate thought was that he was teasing me; however, when it became clear he was absolutely serious, I responded, "Are you Eliphaz, Bildad, or Zophar?"

I had a basic knowledge of the book of *Job*, and this just seemed all too familiar. We visited for a while about the book of *Job*, but about that time the kidney stone decided to change positions. He drove me to the emergency room, still demanding that I confess my sins. At that time I did not understand why Job had lost his wealth and health; I was convinced, however, that Job's problems were not caused by sin. The pain subsided while we were in the ER, and my friend drove me home, frustrated he had not accomplished his mission. However, he may have helped more than he will ever realize because my interest in understanding the book of *Job* definitely increased.

Trying to deal with Marian's problems and my own set of disasters left me with high blood pressure, ulcers, and kidney stones. Imagine my stress level when I learned after four months of living with a cast on my left leg that my leg had not been set correctly, that doctors would have to re-break my leg, and that my body would have to start the healing process all over again.

My dad died in the summer of 1984, and later that year, I realized we could no longer take care of my wife at home. My son Eddie was attending college in Oklahoma; and my two daughters were home—Tammy in high school and Cheri in junior high. I was trying to work as many jobs as possible to make ends meet. As a family we realized the time had come, but still, the trauma of having to place a loved one in a nursing home created one of the biggest alligators I have ever seen. While I felt support from friends who tried to understand what my family was experiencing, I also felt judgment and condemnation from others who had no clue why the nursing home decision was made. The lesson here may be that it is much easier to endure and tolerate pain when it is not your own.

My first wife died in 1987 at the age of 47, after years of struggling through her personal "alligator pond." She maintained her beautiful smile and tremendous faith in God through it all. Her death brought another reality to light: all "alligator pond" experiences come to an end, even if the finale requires death. We learned that death is God's ultimate answer to healing; one receives a new body, not a patched one. After the death of a loved one, life goes on for others who have been sharing the alligator experience. For some, grief becomes a new family of alligators; others may be ready to move on and face other alligators as they appear. Our family was comforted and strengthened by Paul's message:

> *1 Thessalonians 4:13-14: "Brothers, we do not want you to be ignorant about those who fall asleep, or to grieve like the rest of men, who have no hope. We believe that Jesus died and rose again and so we believe that God will bring with Jesus those who have fallen asleep in him."* NIV

Prior to Marian's death, we had been grieving as we watched our loved one going steadily downhill. At the time of her departure, she weighed only 65 pounds. Having looked the possibility of death in the face for years, and after seeing a loved one suffer, our children and I discovered we were still not fully prepared for the end. Our grieving was for ourselves, but relief would appear when we focused on Marian's looking forward to the time her suffering would end.

I remarried in 1988, and my life has been tremendously blessed by another wonderful Christian mate, Wilsie Bilbrey Richardson. I continued teaching at the junior college through academic year 1988-89 before resigning to enter fulltime ministry. I don't believe I would have ever taken this step if it had not been for the alligators of life. A short time after I began full-time ministry, a friend of mine said, "You remind me so much of Job." I responded, "No way! My life is going great!" He said, "That's my point. I'm talking about the end of the story. Your present circumstances after years of difficulty remind me of Job." Once again, my interest in the book of *Job* received a tweak.

After the fog had passed to allow me to see more clearly, I realized that compared to Job, my life had been a cakewalk. The earlier interest I had in Job's suffering took an upswing shortly after I entered the ministry and looked for ways to help others. I have now read the book of *Job* in eight different versions, some more than once, because my love of the book and my desire to remember every detail is strong. It took several years of teaching classes and telling friends about my insights on the book of *Job* to come to the point of being ready to put my thoughts into print. This volume has been arranged in thirteen chapters, to facilitate quarterly studies on the book of *Job*. To further assist Bible classes, each segment is followed by a study guide.

TABLE OF CONTENTS

CHAPTER 1

– UNDERSTANDING THE BOOK OF JOB

Much scholarly work has been written concerning the book of *Job*. After the book has been dissected by so many authors, one thing is certain: much is still unknown and will most likely remain that way. We still don't know who wrote the book or when it was written; furthermore, the question of historicity has never been settled. Was there a real person named Job who lived in a real location called Uz? Where is Uz located? If Job did exist, when did he live? The Bible gives no clue as to the timeframe of *Job*'s experiences. In all actuality, if the answers were available, they could offer nothing to change the deep concepts within the book; consequently, the message of *Job* will be our focus as we look for ways to cope with suffering when our "alligator ponds" arrive.

Focusing on the meaning of the book of *Job*, this volume will not be written as a commentary concerning itself with a verse-by-verse explanation; rather, our time will be spent decoding the deep meaning of the book and examining the complex questions that affect our understanding of suffering.

If one accepts the Bible as authority, the existence of a man named Job becomes very credible when reading the prophecies of Ezekiel. The prophet quotes God as saying,

> *"Son of man, if a country sins against me by being unfaithful and I stretch out my hand against it to cut off its food supply and send famine upon it and kill its men and their animals, even if these three men -- Noah, Daniel and Job -- were in it, they could save only themselves by their righteousness, declares the Sovereign LORD." Ezekiel 14:12-14* NIV

I don't need a birth certificate to believe Job was a real person in history. I don't need to know his genealogical background, location of birth, or other bits of information that might prove to be of interest. It is enough for me to know God spoke about Job in a book other than the one under consideration. Furthermore, the person Job is mentioned in a New Testament book:

> *James 5:11 "As you know, we consider blessed those who have persevered. You have heard of Job's perseverance and have seen what the Lord finally brought about. The Lord is full of compassion and mercy."* NIV

The book of *Job* is included in every collection of books accepted and classified as canonical. It is found in the Jewish collection of 39 books completed over three centuries before the Christian era. About 282 B.C., the Old Testament was translated from Hebrew into Greek in what is called the Septuagint. The book of *Job* was never questioned when the Latin Vulgate, the first Bible containing both the Old and New Testaments, was completed around 400 A.D.

Believing the book of *Job* is credible because of its presence in the Bible, and believing Job was a real person because of his being mentioned in other biblical books, all other wrestling over peripheral issues misses the message. For these reasons, this volume will be more concerned with the ever present theme of human suffering and redemption, in addition to numerous other valuable lessons we might learn from Job's experiences.

.

PITFALLS TO UNDERSTANDING THE BOOK OF *JOB*

1 – Failure to Pray

Without God's guidance, readers are left to their own intelligence, insights, and limitations. I believe prayer to be essential to better understanding of God's will. Hopefully this volume will help with insights to encourage further study of the book of *Job*, but don't forget to pray for God to open doors of understanding.

2 – Preconceived Ideas

Not everything we have been told about the book and about the man is totally accurate. The only Bible I knew during my early years was the King

James Version, and a verse in the book of *James* forever painted a picture of Job's being the epitome of "patience."

> *James 5:11 "Behold, we count them happy which endure. Ye have heard of the patience of Job, and have seen the end of the Lord; that the Lord is very pitiful, and of tender mercy."* KJV

While I came to believe Job to be patient, I never heard or considered the word <u>pitiful</u> as being a characteristic of God. Yet, the same verse in the KJV that makes a statement about Job makes a statement about God as well. When the New Testament was translated into English, the words <u>patience</u> and <u>pitiful</u> had different meanings than they have today. The word <u>patience</u> indicates a willingness to calmly wait for desired results; chapters 3 through 31 of *Job* reveal the feelings of a man who is anything but patient. If one reads the book looking for evidence of Job's patience, the real message will be hard to decipher.

Today, the Greek word, once translated as "patience," is better translated as "perseverance." Job is quite impatient, requesting God's immediate response to his demands; however, it is clear that he does persevere to receive blessings from God. The KJV also indicates God is pitiful.

The word <u>pitiful</u> is clearly understood today as meaning 'wretched' or 'horrible'; these words do not accurately describe God; however, when the first English translations were being made, the word <u>pitiful</u> meant "full of pity." Rather than translating the Greek word as "pitiful," most modern translations, including the New King James Version, use some form of the word "compassionate." We can all be thankful God is compassionate rather than pitiful. If one is to understand the book of *Job*, he or she must back up and approach the subject with an open mind to understanding truth about the man Job. Scripture will reveal that he is not patient at all; however, he is certainly steadfast, and he does persevere!

3 – Relying on only one Bible version

In today's world, one can seek insights through various versions of the Bible that are readily available. One can even purchase computer Bible programs to see the same verse paralleled in several versions on one screen. The internet also offers the possibility of paralleling a verse to see how it has been worded by various translators. One of the most valuable books in my library is the Bible in twenty-five versions. It's obviously a little larger Bible than most, but the book uses the King James as the main text, and any major variation of a verse is noted along with the abbreviation of the version. This book has served as one of the best commentaries in my library.

By reading various versions, one's comprehension can be enhanced by different words and phrases. I grew up reading the King James Version, and my Sunday school teachers were reading, studying, and teaching from the same version. Because of my background, to this day when a verse comes to mind and I quote the material, most of the time I will be quoting the KJV. While I have a love for the Old English, I also realize that the language doesn't help one comprehend to the highest level.

The use of the word patience and the word pitiful, as indicated earlier, give strong evidence that archaic language hinders accurate understanding. The comparison below parallels the KJV with the New Jerusalem Bible, a version developed in Britain. British spellings sometimes vary, so whenever the NJB is used, I will make adjustments to conform to American spellings. While the spelling is adjusted, the word itself will not be changed. Consider the difference in wording on the following two verses:

King James Version	New Jerusalem Bible
Job 36:15-17	*Job 36:15-17*
He delivereth the poor in his affliction, and openeth their ears in oppression. Even so would he have removed thee out of the strait into a broad place, where there is no straitness; and that which should be set on thy table should be full of fatness. But thou hast fulfilled the judgment of the wicked: judgment and justice take hold on thee.	*But God saves the afflicted by his affliction, warning him in his misery. You, too, he would like to snatch from torment. While you were enjoying boundless abundance, with rich food piled high on your table, you did not bring the wicked to trial and did not give fair judgment to the orphan.*

Did these three short verses seem a little clearer in the NJB? More will be said concerning these verses later in this volume, but for now this author is illustrating that different wording brings different understanding. This volume will utilize several versions to help the reader see the beauty of

4

reading other versions for clarity and comprehension. Below is a list of the versions used in this volume; the abbreviations will be used to identify the particular translation used at the time:

ASV – American Standard Version

BBE – Bible in Basic English

ESV – English Standard Version

GNT – Good News Testament

KJV – King James Version

LB – Living Bible

NAS – New American Standard

NASU – New American Standard Updated

NCV – New Century Version

NET – New English Testament

NJB – New Jerusalem Bible

NIV – New International Version

NKJV – New King James Version

NLT – New Living Testament

NRS – New Revised Standard

RSV – Revised Standard Version

TM – The Message

TNIV – Today's New International Version

4 – Bad Reading/Study Habits

Most of us read limited amounts of a Bible book at one sitting; a chapter or two today, a little more tomorrow, and a couple on day three. Each time we resume our reading, the previous material has been clouded to a degree by passing time and inaccurate recall. This reality became very evident to me a few years ago when we were traveling from Texas to Oregon. Sometime before, we had agreed on a goal of reading the Bible through each year; to further our understanding, reading from a new version each year.

This particular year we were reading the New Jerusalem Bible. My wife, Wilsie, was driving at the time, and I verbally read the book of *Job* from beginning to end without a break in the action. Because of the non-stop reading from a new version, the book of *Job* came alive like never before. When we concluded our reading, I said, "For the first time in my life, I believe I understand the message in this book. Let me tell you what I see, and then let's talk." I knew I had to write a book at some time, but it took a while for the message of *Job* to grow. I hope and pray this volume will present a few insights and will raise enough questions to encourage the reading of the book of *Job* in one sitting.

By praying, putting aside preconceived ideas, using a different version, and reading the entire book in one day, the possibility of understanding *Job* will be much greater. To assist your study of the book of *Job*, I have found three keys to comprehension.

KEYS TO UNDERSTANDING THE BOOK OF *JOB*

1 – Trust the Narrator from the beginning to the end

Since the entire story of Job's suffering is told by a Narrator, it is important to accept every statement the Narrator makes in analyzing the characters and circumstances involved. Because of reliance on a Narrator who has no name, throughout this volume I have used the upper case "N" to treat the word <u>Narrator</u> like a name. Many people pay attention to what the Narrator has to say in the first two chapters, but somehow the Narrator's further information and insights get lost in a maze of speeches by Job and his three friends. If we trust the Narrator in the first part of the book, we must also trust the Narrator in the middle of the book and at the end of the book. Keep this thought in mind as an overview, and the message of *Job* will be easier to comprehend. The Narrator's description of Job toward the end of the book is one-hundred-eighty degrees from the description in the first two chapters of *Job*.

In the first chapter of *Job*, the Narrator paints a glowing picture of Job's character; however, the same Narrator has quite a different description in chapter 32 after the debate between Job and friends comes to an end. Notice this contrast in the next two verses. If we trust the Narrator in chapter 1, what do we do with chapter 32?

> *Job 1:1 In the land of Uz there lived a man whose name was Job. This man was blameless and upright; he feared God and shunned evil.* NIV

> *Job 32:1 So these three men stopped answering Job, because he was righteous in his own eyes.* NIV

How and why does Job's description change so drastically in the Narrator's eyes? This volume will explore the text to find the answer.

2 – Pay attention to Elihu

Elihu is the fourth character who seems to appear out of nowhere; most authors make light of Elihu as being an egotistical, young know it all. Later in this volume, two chapters will highlight Elihu for the following reasons:

1) Neither Job nor his friends ever deny, refute, or even respond to anything Elihu has to say.
2) Elihu makes statements about himself that would have been absolute heresy if not true.
3) When God arrives to pass judgment, He chastises Job, Eliphaz, Bildad, and Zophar, but He says nothing to correct the words of Elihu.
4) Elihu previews the very things God has to say concerning Job's arrogance.
5) Deeper study and analysis will prove that Elihu is the main key for understanding the book of *Job*.

3 – God is Supreme

Job learns through his suffering and through his encounter with the Almighty that he is not God, nor is he equal to God in any respect. When God speaks in chapters 38 through 42, He makes His sovereignty known in undeniable terms. God made the universe, and only He knows how and why everything works in its own special way.

Furthermore, Satan is not another god with powers possessed only by the Almighty. Satan is not omnipotent, nor omniscient, nor does he have the power of omnipresence. Satan does not approach God and reveal his desire to pollute the life of Job; God draws Satan's attention to Job and sends him to make Job's life miserable. God does not give Satan unlimited range to disrupt Job's life; be aware that God sets the parameters for the suffering that will take place. Simply put, the book of *Job* is **NOT** about a struggle between God and Satan over the soul of Job. Chapter one will explore God's use of angels in furthering His work, and we will explore how God unleashes evil forces to accomplish His purposes.

SIGNIFICANCE OF THE BOOK OF *JOB*

At some point in life, everyone faces personal disasters of various types; the ultimate outcome of such crises depends on how one copes through the trauma. How can one face the loss of property or an occupation? Even worse, how does one deal with serious physical problems suffered by self, family members, or close friends? When one faces the death of a spouse, parent, sibling, or child, life may be hard to bear. Some never seem to get past the grieving process.

When tragedies are running rampant, people face greater possibility of ulcers, high blood pressure, angina, heart attacks, or strokes. One's immune system seems to go into hibernation, and accidents are much more likely; things just seem to stack on top of each other.

The universal nature of tragedy manifests itself in one of the following scenarios: 1) One is currently entering an alligator pond experience; 2) One is in the middle of misfortune; 3) One has completed an "alligator pond" debacle; 4) One has alligators lurking to strike in the future. To live is to suffer! But how do we make it through the suffering? I hope and pray this material will help you persevere through whatever "alligator ponds" you may encounter.

STUDY GUIDE – Chapter 1

1. Does "alligator pond" adequately describe life's struggles?

2. Is the book of *Job* historical truth or is it an allegory?

3. How important is prayer in understanding the Bible?

4. Have you ever changed a perception when reading a different version?

5. How can different versions benefit study?

6. What is your Bible version of choice and why?

7. How important is the Narrator in the book of *Job*?

8. What have you been taught in the past concerning Elihu?

CHAPTER 2

– HELL'S ANGEL ARRIVES

God's use of angels, both good and bad

Human eyes see what is taking place in the physical realm, but at times it becomes obvious that things are happening in ways we cannot understand or explain. The book of *Hebrews* has something to say about God's work through angel servants.

> *Hebrews 1:14   Are not all angels ministering spirits, sent to serve those who will inherit salvation?* TNIV

> *Hebrews 13:2-3   Don't forget to show hospitality to strangers, for some who have done this have entertained angels without realizing it!* NLT

These passages help students of the book of *Job* understand why angels appear before God to receive their work schedules for the day. We know that God uses good angels to minister to His servants, but for some reason, there is also an evil realm of angels at work. The apostle Paul explains angel warfare in this way:

> *Ephesians 6:10-14   Finally, be strong in the Lord, and in the strength of His might. Put on the full armor of God, that you may be able to stand firm against the schemes of the devil. For our struggle is not against flesh and blood, but against the rulers, against the powers, against the world forces of this darkness, against the spiritual forces of wickedness in the heavenly places. Therefore, take up the full armor of God, that you may be able to resist in the evil day, and having done everything, to stand firm.* NASB

It is important to remember at all times that God is sovereign and rules over the entirety of His creation. Scripture presents a basic truth: God can and does use evil to accomplish His purposes.

> *Judges 9:23 And God sent an evil spirit between Abimelech and the men of Shechem; and the men of Shechem dealt treacherously with Abimelech.* RSV

> *1 Samuel 16:14 Now the Spirit of the Lord had departed from Saul, and an evil spirit from the Lord tormented him.* NIV

> *1 Samuel 19:9-10 But an evil spirit from the Lord came upon Saul as he was sitting in his house with his spear in his hand. While David was playing the harp, Saul tried to pin him to the wall with his spear, but David eluded him as Saul drove the spear into the wall.* NIV

The Bible portrays Satan's actions in two ways; one pictures Satan as a roaring lion, roaming the earth to seek those he can destroy.

> *1 Peter 5:8-9 Be sober, be vigilant; because your adversary the devil walks about like a roaring lion, seeking whom he may devour. Resist him, steadfast in the faith, knowing that the same sufferings are experienced by your brotherhood in the world.* NKJV

On the other hand, Satan and his evil angels are described as being locked in chains, giving the impression that Satan is unable to roam the earth in his search for victims.

> *Jude 1:6 And the angels who did not keep their own position, but left their proper dwelling, he has kept in eternal chains in deepest darkness for the judgment of the great day.* NRS

The apostle Peter confirms the statement above in *2 Peter 2:4*. Satan is one of those evil angels, but how do we harmonize Satan's roaming the earth while being bound by chains at the same time? God's sovereignty explains the apparent dilemma; God has Satan on a chain, the length of which He controls. Who would want to go anywhere near a lion, even if the lion is chained to protect people? Those within the vicinity of a chained lion are protected as long as they remain further away than the length of the chain.

However, people have free will and can choose to enter the lion's territory with the threat of being eaten alive. Scripture never leaves any doubt as to who is in control! God keeps Satan on a chain, and He gives Satan permission to strike Job's wealth and health. The disasters could move Job either direction, but Job perseveres through the trials to make the right decision.

> *1 Corinthians 10:13 No temptation has overtaken you that is not common to man. God is faithful, and he will not let you be tempted beyond your strength, but with the temptation will also provide the way of escape, that you may be able to endure it.* RSV

God has the final destiny of Satan and his angels arranged, and the sovereignty of God will prevail in the end.

> *Matthew 25:41 "Then He will also say to those on His left, 'Depart from Me, accursed ones, into the eternal fire which has been prepared for the devil and his angels.'"* NASB

> *Revelation 20:10 Then the devil, who led them astray, was hurled into the lake of fire and sulfur, where the beast and the false prophet are, and their torture will not come to an end, day or night, for ever and ever.* NJB

At times God uses evil to bring about certain events that further His cause. This becomes evident when God teaches King David and Israel the need to trust in the Lord. David decides that the Israelite army must be counted to see whether they have enough troops to advance against the enemy. Joab, his commander-in-chief, urges David to forgo the numbering of the troops, but David cannot be dissuaded. God's use of the powers of Satan moves David into a drastic error of judgment. Check the scriptures below to see that God uses evil to His desired ends.

> *1 Chronicles 21:1 Satan rose up against Israel and incited David to take a census of Israel.* NIV

> *2 Samuel 24:1 The anger of the Lord burned against Israel, and he incited David against them, saying, "Go and take a census of Israel and Judah."* NIV

Does Satan incite David to take the census, or does God incite David to do it? I jokingly say the answer is "Yes!" God uses Satan to incite David to bring about a result that will serve His purpose of ultimately having a sacrifice made on the very site that will become the home of the Temple of Israel.

With these concepts in mind, it makes more sense that Satan (an evil angel) comes before God at times to receive orders just as the other angels do. God asks, "Have you considered my servant Job?" The New Jerusalem Bible words it this way:

> *Job 1:8 So Yahweh asked him, "Did you pay any attention to my servant Job? There is no one like him on the earth: a sound and honest man who fears God and shuns evil."* NJB

Satan responds that there is no point in spending time and effort on Job, because God has blessed him and has put a hedge of protection around him. Why bother? Why isn't God pleased that this upright man is so good that even Satan leaves him alone? Wouldn't you expect God to say, "That's right, and the hedge is going to stay; you leave my faithful servant alone!" But this is not the case; God sends Satan on a mission with limits on the boundaries of attack, proving that God controls Satan and evil.

Satan firmly believes Job will curse God to His face if the hedge is removed. God extends the boundaries for attack, and Satan takes his job seriously by going to the absolute limit of his chains. The boundary is wide; Satan can destroy everything Job possesses, but he is to do no harm to Job's person. What wild disasters Satan creates! Job loses all his oxen, donkeys, sheep, and camels in one day; in addition, he loses his 10 children and all but four of his servants. Does God do this for no purpose other than to see if He can win a contest with Satan? We can cancel that thought because of God's second conversation with Satan.

> *Job 2:3 Yahweh asked him, "Did you pay any attention to my servant Job? There is no one like him on the earth: a sound and honest man who fears God and shuns evil. He persists in his integrity still; you achieved nothing by provoking me to ruin him."* NJB

God is seeking an outcome from Satan's efforts, or the last statement would make no sense. Job's losses do not provide the result God hopes to achieve. Satan guarantees that Job will curse God to His face if he suffers to the point of death. I do not believe God intends that Job curse Him, but God does intend to get some unknown result, so He sends Satan on his second mission. The first parameters set on Satan's "considering" Job leaves Satan unable to attack Job's person. However, God takes the barrier down and leaves a wide-open boundary with the only requirement being that Job remains alive. Anything else would fit within Satan's commission, and he takes advantage of it by striking Job's entire body,

> *Job 2:7 So Satan left the presence of Yahweh. He struck Job down with malignant ulcers from the sole of his foot to the top of his head.* NJB

Once again, Satan's efforts fail to gain immediate results, because Job still maintains his integrity by not saying anything negative about God.

> *Job 2:10 "... Shall we accept good from God, and not trouble?" In all this, Job did not sin in what he said.* NIV

The text does not tell us how long it took the three friends of Job to arrive. Despite not having email, the three friends learn about his demise and go to offer their advice. As Eliphaz, Bildad, and Zophar approach Job's home, they see him from a distance, but he is so disfigured they don't recognize him. For seven days all sit with no sound heard except for the moaning taking place; the losses have been so massive that all sit in stunned silence. Finally Job breaks the ice. Observe what he has to say:

> *Job 3:1 At last Job spoke, and cursed the day of his birth.* LB

Satan's work accomplishes a change in Job, a change that will have to run its course before Job can get his feet on the ground again. At the end of the book, God's efforts through Satan's destructive means will prove fruitful.

If Job does not sin by lashing out at God after the first round of losses, and if Job does not sin through making negative comments about God after being covered with ulcerous sores over his entire body, what is Job doing from chapter 3 through 31?

As chapter 3 opens, the reader gets a glimpse of Job's new direction of conversation. Job begins railing against God for treating him unfairly. Is this the result God is seeking? It must have been, because God does not use Satan any further; it is time now for the disasters to work whatever effects

God is seeking. Before we complete the discussion concerning Satan's work, there is one more verse that will absolutely prove that God is the One who brings disaster on Job by using the evils of Satan. The Narrator, whom we trust, makes the following comment:

> *Job 42:11 Then all his brothers, all his sisters, and all those who had been his acquaintances before, came to him and ate food with him in his house; and they consoled him and comforted him for all the adversity that the Lord had brought upon him. Each one gave him a piece of silver and each a ring of gold.* NKJ

Now that evidence has been presented to prove God uses Satan's powers of destruction to affect Job in some way, the next chapter of this volume will cover the subject of suffering. Why is it necessary for Job to suffer, and what does this information mean to modern day followers of God?

STUDY GUIDE – Chapter 2

1. How important are angels in the lives of humans?

2. How has God used evil to accomplish His purposes?

3. What is the significance of evil angels being in chains?

4. What was the point of God's question, "Have you considered my servant Job"?

5. Why has Satan left Job alone before God asks the question?

6. How do you assess Job's immediate responses after Satan's two attacks?

7. Discuss Job's attitude change as *Job 3* opens.

8. Is the book of Job a struggle between God and Satan for Job's soul?

CHAPTER 3

– LORD, WHY ME?

Job loses great wealth and health.

In reading the book of *Job*, one can make a totally safe conclusion— Job's losses are about as bad as it gets! Major disasters have left others in difficult straits with losses of all possessions, family, and health; however, it would be hard to find anyone who surpasses the magnitude of traumatic events encountered by the patriarch Job.

In *Job 1*, God solicits the assistance of Satan to alter Job's circumstances; Job had been thoroughly blessed in the first part of his life, but things were about to change. As mentioned in the previous chapter of this volume, God sends Satan to attack all Job possesses, but He forbids Satan's laying a finger on Job's person. The text reveals the results of Satan's first attack on Job:

> *Job 1:13-19 One day when his sons and daughters were eating and drinking wine in the eldest brother's house, a messenger came to Job and said, "The oxen were plowing and the donkeys were feeding beside them, and the Sabeans fell on them and carried them off, and killed the servants with the edge of the sword; I alone have escaped to tell you." While he was still speaking, another came and said, "The fire of God fell from heaven and burned up the sheep and the servants, and consumed them; I alone have escaped to tell you." While he was still speaking, another came and said, "The Chaldeans formed three columns, made a raid on the camels and carried them off, and killed the servants with the edge of the sword; I alone have escaped to tell you." While he was still speaking, another came and said, "Your*

sons and daughters were eating and drinking wine in their eldest brother's house, and suddenly a great wind came across the desert, struck the four corners of the house, and it fell on the young people, and they are dead; I alone have escaped to tell you." NRS

When confronted with news of unthinkable magnitude, Job accepts the losses, praises God, and says nothing negative concerning God's providence.

Job 1:20-22 At this, Job got up and tore his robe and shaved his head. Then he fell to the ground in worship and said: "Naked I came from my mother's womb, and naked I will depart. The Lord gave and the Lord has taken away; may the name of the Lord be praised." In all this, Job did not sin by charging God with wrongdoing. NIV

It becomes apparent that God is seeking different results when He says to Satan, "He still maintains his integrity, though you incited me against him to ruin him without any reason." Translation: "You said Job would break if his possessions were lost, and I sent you to do it. What you have done did not break Job's spirit." God is not through trying to adjust Job's attitude; He once again commissions Satan to encounter Job. This time God allows Satan to "lay a finger" on Job, but, once again, He limits Satan's freedom and chain length by forbidding him to take Job's life. Anything short of death would be permissible, so Satan once again goes to the furthest extent of his chain by inflicting sores over ALL of Job's body.

Job 2:7-10 Then Satan went out from the presence of the LORD and smote Job with sore boils from the sole of his foot to the crown of his head. And he took a potsherd to scrape himself while he was sitting among the ashes. Then his wife said to him, Do you still hold fast your integrity? Curse God and die!" But he said to her, "You speak as one of the foolish women speaks. Shall we indeed accept good from God and not accept adversity?" In all this Job did not sin with his lips. NASU

Having sores over his entire body, there is no way Job can find relief. The sores on the soles of his feet make standing unbearable; he cannot lie down without experiencing horrors. He cannot even stand on his head to escape the pain. To make matters worse, his wife cajoles him for not cursing God. The reader is left puzzling over the response of Job's wife. We might hope she empathizes with Job to the fullest, heartsick of all that has befallen her husband; however, it is possible she has become cynical.

For some reason unknown to the reader, God has left Job's wife alive, and the Narrator says nothing else about her. Coupled with earlier losses, readers are amazed that Job continues his refusal to blame God for his suffering.

Job's upright nature is apparent as he refuses to blame God after losing his sheep, camels, donkeys, servants, and all ten children. His demeanor continues for seven days after Satan strikes him with sores covering his entire body. Job's refusal to denounce his circumstances ends as *Job 3* opens. From chapter 3 through 31, Job's confusion, anger, and insistence on his goodness, along with demands issued to God, flow from his mouth.

Just as Job wonders why these things have come his way, we often ask the same questions: Why me? Why now? What have I done to deserve this? What is God up to? Two major questions need to be explored: 1) Why does mankind suffer? 2) How should one respond to suffering?

WHY DOES MANKIND SUFFER?

As four reasons for human suffering are examined, keep in mind that these reasons are not mutually exclusive, so two or more may be operating at the same time. One may be suffering punishment for specific sinful behavior, but at the same time God may be using His discipline to mold His child into a more productive path of life. With this parameter in mind, let's examine different reasons why we all go through suffering from time-to-time.

1. Man's foolish actions lead to suffering.

When Adam and Eve broke God's law by eating from the Tree of Knowledge of Good and Evil, they were punished with pain and suffering, that ultimately resulted in death. They did not drop dead the instant they sinned, but apparently their cells began to die at that moment. Later in *Genesis*, Cain killed his brother Abel and was punished because of his evil actions.

Genesis 4:10-11 The Lord said, "What have you done? Listen! Your brother's blood cries out to me from the ground. Now you are under a curse and driven from the ground, which opened its mouth to receive your brother's blood from your hand." NIV

The lesson of the two trees in the Garden of Eden is simple: mankind always has a choice of two ways of life. One can walk in the path of the Tree of Life, or one can choose to live seeking the tree of knowledge of good and evil. No human being is strong enough to follow the way of life consistently; consequently, we each make decisions throughout life, choosing which tree on which to nibble. Choosing the wrong path of life has consequences that are painful and sometimes the pain is quite severe.

Romans 3:21-24 But God has a way to make people right with him without the law, and he has now shown us that way which the law and the prophets told us about. God makes people right with himself through their faith in Jesus Christ. This is true for all who believe in Christ, because all people are the same: Everyone has sinned and fallen short of God's glorious standard, and all need to be made right with God by his grace, which is a free gift. They need to be made free from sin through Jesus Christ. NCV

1 John 1:8-10 If we claim we have no sin, we are only fooling ourselves and not living in the truth. But if we confess our sins to him, he is faithful and just to forgive us our sins and to cleanse us from all wickedness. If we claim we have not sinned, we are calling God a liar and showing that his word has no place in our hearts. NLT

Eliphaz, Bildad, and Zophar believe Job's secret sin is the absolute reason for his suffering. Yes, they know that Job's life appears squeaky clean, yet (they reason), Job must be hiding something to bring about those horrendous losses. Because the Narrator knows Job has lived a life above reproach, he says Job is "blameless." In fact God also tells Satan that Job is "blameless and upright; there is no one in the land like Job." It's easy to see why Job's friends think his sins are plaguing his life when we read verses like the following:

Galatians 6:7-8 Don't be misled: No one makes a fool of God. What a person plants, he will harvest. The person who plants selfishness, ignoring the needs of others — ignoring God! — harvests a crop of weeds. All he'll have to show for his life is weeds! But the one who plants in response to God, letting God's Spirit do the growth work in him, harvests a crop of real life, eternal life. TM

We have all witnessed the devastation of venereal disease, AIDS, sclerosis of the liver, and other maladies caused by life-style choices. Job has not lived life on the wild side, so he refutes their accusations and insists on his innocence. Job's three friends cannot furnish empirical evidence of his breaking any rule or any law. Eliphaz asserts that Job has committed specific sins, but God later chastises all three friends for their misfired attempts to blame Job of breaking rules.

None of Job's actions have been illegal; however, an attitude of arrogance and not doing what is right is just as sinful as doing something wrong! I remember years ago hearing prayers asking God to forgive our "sins of omission and commission." As a child, I did not understand what this jargon meant; this prayer language has disappeared, but it referred to sinful acts and to failure to do what is right. It is possible to keep all rules and regulations and still sin by not doing good deeds. Job is correct in believing he has committed no sins of "commission." After all, God has declared Job to be an upright and blameless man, but Job has sins of "omission" in failing to humble himself before God and his neighbors.

Another thought: If sin is paid back in-kind by punishment, this would simplify the situation. When suffering, one would know his or her actions created the problem; every sin would bring punishment equal to the transgression.

2. Everyone suffers because of living in a world infected by sin.

Viruses spread without respect of persons, and the chemicals with which we live often become our enemies. Despite hand sanitizers, disease is still passed from one person to another, and the diseases often occur in epidemic proportions. A tsunami sweeps across the land turning it into an ocean, or a tornado rips through a community leaving what appears to be a battle field in which all residents suffer losses. Fires spread across an area, destroying life and property.

Scripture makes it perfectly clear that all suffering is a by-product and consequent of sin. Original sin led to death for all who are born of man, and original sin led to pain and suffering. Eve was the first to eat the "forbidden fruit," and her punishment was described in this way:

> *Genesis 3:16 To the woman he said, "I will greatly multiply your pain in childbearing; in pain you shall bring forth children, yet your desire shall be for your husband, and he shall rule over you."* RSV

All mothers from that day forward have experienced extreme pain in child-birth, not because of personal sin, but because we live in a sinful world. Adam was present when Eve nibbled the fruit; he could have intervened, but he chose to allow it and to participate in some nibbling of his own. Adam's punishment has carried over to every person who has ever lived on earth.

> *Genesis 3:17-19 And to Adam he said, "Because you have listened to the voice of your wife and have eaten of the tree of which I commanded you, 'You shall not eat of it,' cursed is the ground because of you; in toil you shall eat of it all the days of your life; thorns and thistles it shall bring forth to you; and you shall eat the plants of the field. In the sweat of your face you shall eat bread till you return to the ground, for out of it you were taken; you are dust, and to dust you shall return."* RSV

The Bible also teaches that children and grandchildren are often affected by the sins of their parents; they experience punishment for things they did not do. However, living in this old sinful world, we have all seen this phenomenon play out.

> *Exodus 34:7 He does not leave the guilty unpunished; he punishes the children and their children for the sin of the fathers to the third and fourth generation."* NIV

When God commissioned Moses to lead the exodus of Israel from Egypt to give them the land of Canaan, sin prevented their entrance. Ten of the twelve spies returned with a negative report, discouraging the entire

24

community. Believing the report about giants living in the land, the people complained about their plight. There may have been some who did not believe the report, and there were children who had nothing to do with the complaining. Despite the inactivity of some, all were made to suffer. Sometimes entire communities, states, and nations suffer because the actions of their leaders place all within harm's way. This is exactly what happened to the Israelites.

> *Numbers 14:34-35 For forty years — one year for each of the forty days you explored the land — you will suffer for your sins and know what it is like to have me against you.' NIV*

Could this be the cause of Job's suffering? In a roundabout way it may have played in his suffering; however, the intense suffering and absolute losses indicate there is something more to Job's suffering than merely living in a sinful world. God's commissioning of Satan and singling out Job also points to a different conclusion. In understanding our own suffering, this reason should always be considered. WARNING: We should not let this possibility blind us to our personal sins that may be contributing to our own pain and anguish.

3. Some suffer because of their beliefs and religious convictions.

> *1 Peter 2:19-22 For this finds favor, if for the sake of conscience toward God a man bears up under sorrows when suffering unjustly. For what credit is there if, when you sin and are harshly treated, you endure it with patience? But if when you do what is right and suffer for it you patiently endure it, this finds favor with God. For you have been called for this purpose, since Christ also suffered for you, leaving you an example for you to follow in His steps. NASB*

The apostle Paul, who endured much pain and anguish, guarantees that suffering will come to those who live godly lives in the service of Jesus Christ.

> *2 Timothy 3:12-13 But anybody who tries to live in devotion to Christ is certain to be persecuted; while these*

wicked impostors will go from bad to worse, deceiving others, and themselves deceived. NJB

Many are suffering throughout the world today because of their faith in Jesus Christ and their desire to live godly lives. In the Islamic world, Christians are currently being persecuted in Nigeria, Pakistan, Somalia, Egypt, and Iran. In the Far East, Christians are suffering in Indonesia, China, and Mongolia. As I am writing this material, persecution is also occurring in India, and evangelical Christians are being persecuted in the Puebla State of Mexico. Signs of coming persecution can be seen in the United States of America, and the test of faith and commitment may be on the way.

Job is not being persecuted because of his faith; God is the one who sanctions the attacks and sets the parameters for the events that follow.

4. God sometimes disciplines to encourage growth and change in one's life.

God's directed punishment may be delivered because of sin; however, sometimes God brings suffering to help His saints mature. Remember that it rains on the just and the unjust. What is it that God is seeking from the pain and anguish of His followers? After the sins of King David brought one disaster upon another to his household, David realized what God was really trying to accomplish.

> *Psalms 51:17 The sacrifices of God are a broken spirit; a broken and contrite heart, O God, you will not despise.* NIV

The writer of *Hebrews* proclaims there is a difference between God's punishment and God's discipline. Regardless of the cause for our suffering, if we treat our discomfort and inconveniences as God's attempt to mold us into stronger Christians, our reactions are much more in tune with where we need to be.

> *Hebrews 12:4-7 In your struggle against sin you have not yet resisted to the point of shedding your blood. And you have forgotten the exhortation that addresses you as children--"My child, do not regard lightly the discipline of the Lord, or lose heart when you are punished by him; for the Lord disciplines those whom he loves, and chastises every child whom he accepts." Endure trials for the sake of*

discipline. God is treating you as children; for what child is there whom a parent does not discipline? NAS

Whatever the cause of one's suffering, lessons can be learned, and one's relationship with God can be strengthened. It's easy to flash anger during suffering if one sees it as punishment; however, the apostle Peter tells readers that faith can grow when one is tested in the fires of pain.

1 Peter 1:7 These [trials] have come so that your faith — of greater worth than gold, which perishes even though refined by fire — may be proved genuine and may result in praise, glory and honor when Jesus Christ is revealed. NIV

Can you see Job in the scenario presented in the two previous scriptures? Job experiences pain beyond imagination. It is certainly not pleasant, but it is for Job's own benefit the suffering takes place. At the end of it all, Job responds in righteous ways, giving proof he has been trained by his experience. No wonder he receives a great harvest after enduring his training! Job is not being persecuted because of his sins; he is chastised and kept alive in an attempt to bring greater blessings his way. Closer examination of the book of *Job* will help us discover the change God is seeking in his servant Job.

HOW SHOULD ONE RESPOND TO SUFFERING?

Responses to suffering will vary from person-to-person, based on the perceived cause. One person may suffer because of his own blunders, but others may suffer simply because they live in a sin-infested location. Scripture teaches that those who live godly lives will suffer persecution, so what is the cause for my suffering?

1. What should one do when personal sin wrecks lives?

If a person realizes his foolish decisions have brought about the pain and anguish he is encountering, he needs to confess, repent, and pray for God's forgiveness. Too many times people who have ruined their own lives live in denial of the fact; as long as this takes place, relief cannot come, and further emotional trauma is likely. Listen to King David when he realized the need to acknowledge and deal with his sins.

Psalms 32:1-5 How blessed is he whose transgression is forgiven, whose sin is covered! How blessed is the man to whom the Lord does not impute iniquity, and in whose spirit there is no deceit! When I kept silent about my sin, my body wasted away through my groaning all day long. For day and night Your hand was heavy upon me; my vitality was drained away as with the fever heat of summer. Selah. I acknowledged my sin to You, and my iniquity I did not hide; I said, "I will confess my transgressions to the Lord," and You forgave the guilt of my sin. NASU

As mentioned earlier, one may be suffering for more reasons than just one. David was punished for what he had done, but God was also molding David into His kind of person. The apostle Paul, in his apology at Pisidian Antioch, presented a little history lesson in which he made this statement about David.

Acts 13:22 After removing Saul, he made David their king. He testified concerning him: 'I have found David son of Jesse a man after my own heart; he will do everything I want him to do.' NIV

David was one who took responsibility for his mistakes and accepted the results that came his way. After the turmoil he experienced because of his sins, David realized God's mercy spared him from getting what he deserved.

Job never appeals to God for mercy; rather, he accuses God of wrong doing and calls for justice because he perceives himself to be in the right. Compare this attitude with David's acknowledgement of God's mercy:

Psalms 103:9-10 The Lord is merciful and gracious, Slow to anger, and abounding in mercy. He will not always strive with us, nor will He keep His anger forever. He has not dealt with us according to our sins, nor punished us according to our iniquities. NJB

Moral: If sinful decisions lead to suffering, one must seek forgiveness and find ways to change the direction of his or her life.

2. How should one respond to suffering caused by living in a sin infected world?

When a virus strikes in epidemic proportions, or when a tornado wipes out an entire city, what should be the response of those who suffer losses? I remember driving through Lubbock in 1970 as I traveled with my high school debate team to the national speech tournament. In a neighborhood where every house had been leveled, one family had put a sign in the front yard that read, "These are mere trinkets; praise the Lord we are all alive." Perhaps the family had learned from the words of James:

> *James 1:2-4   Consider it a sheer gift, friends, when tests and challenges come at you from all sides.   You know that under pressure, your faith-life is forced into the open and shows its true colors.   So don't try to get out of anything prematurely.   Let it do its work so you become mature and well-developed, not deficient in any way.*   TM

After all his suffering, the apostle Paul had something similar to say when he wrote to the church in Rome:

> *Romans 5:3-5 We also rejoice in our sufferings, because we know that suffering produces perseverance; perseverance, character; and character, hope.   And hope does not disappoint us, because God has poured out his love into our hearts by the Holy Spirit, whom he has given us.* NIV

The best thing we can do when there are no answers to the suffering is to determine what can be done to serve God from wherever we find ourselves. How can I go forward from here? When I was going through my worst days of suffering, I was blessed when I was able to assist others who were suffering through an "alligator pond." Thinking of the needs of others helps immensely in reducing the pain and suffering one is encountering.

3. How should one respond when suffering for his or her faith?

I do not pretend to understand the depth of meaning found in the scripture below. Jesus was perfect in the beginning; He was perfect throughout His entire stay on earth, and He is perfect today. However, the writer of *Hebrews* indicates that we need to learn obedience in the face of suffering by following the example of Jesus. Though Jesus was and forever is God, He was incarnated as a man in order to illustrate the need for humans to submit to God's authority. What an example!

> *Hebrews 5:8-10 Although He was a Son, He learned obedience from the things which He suffered. And having been made perfect, He became to all those who obey Him the source of eternal salvation, being designated by God as a high priest according to the order of Melchizedek.* NASU

Jesus prayed for the "cup" (his impending crucifixion) to pass from him, but He continued His prayer saying, "However, Your will be done on earth as it is in heaven." Jesus' human nature gave way to the needs of the Spirit. If one thinks of the suffering Jesus endured because He loved mankind, an acceptance of pain is more likely. Jesus died that we might live. Nails did not hold Jesus to the cross; He said he could call twelve legions of angels to end the ordeal, but love held Him to the cross. And the same great Love resurrected Him from the bonds of the grave.

There's nothing I could go through to equal Jesus' suffering. However, I can decide to endure suffering as a Christian to share in the pain and anguish endured by my Savior. The old song was beautiful that said, "Must Jesus bear the cross alone, and all the world go free? No! There's a cross for everyone, and there's a cross for me." Peter voices this idea in the following passage:

> *1 Peter 4:12-19 Beloved, do not be surprised at the fiery ordeal among you, which comes upon you for your testing, as though some strange thing were happening to you; but to the degree that you share the sufferings of Christ, keep on rejoicing; so that also at the revelation of His glory, you may rejoice with exultation. If you are reviled for the name of Christ, you are blessed, because the Spirit of glory and of God rests upon you. By no means let any of you suffer as a murderer, or thief, or evildoer, or a troublesome meddler; but if anyone suffers as a Christian, let him not feel ashamed, but in that name let him glorify God. For it is time for judgment to begin with the household of God; and if it begins with us first, what will be the outcome for those who do not obey the gospel of God? And if it is with difficulty*

that the righteous is saved, what will become of the godless man and the sinner? Therefore, let those also who suffer according to the will of God entrust their souls to a faithful Creator in doing what is right. NAS

4. How should one respond to suffering intended to bring growth?

Job's suffering comes about because of God's disciplinary measures in attempting to humble an arrogant man. More evidence will be furnished later in this volume to prove without a doubt that Job's pride was his problem. When one is able to get past enough time and through enough stages of grief, it is possible to create a new attitude toward the events. The key is being able to reflect on what Jesus has done for all mankind through His suffering; this change of attitude is explained in the following passages:

> *Hebrews 12:8-13 If you do not have that discipline in which all children share, then you are illegitimate and not his children. Moreover, we had human parents to discipline us, and we respected them. Should we not be even more willing to be subject to the Father of spirits and live? For they disciplined us for a short time as seemed best to them, but he disciplines us for our good, in order that we may share his holiness. Now, discipline always seems painful rather than pleasant at the time, but later it yields the peaceful fruit of righteousness to those who have been trained by it. Therefore lift your drooping hands and strengthen your weak knees, and make straight paths for your feet, so that what is lame may not be put out of joint, but rather be healed.* NRS

> *1 Peter 1:6-7 Be glad about this, even though it may now be necessary for you to be sad for a while because of the many kinds of trials you suffer. Their purpose is to prove that your faith is genuine. Even gold, which can be destroyed, is tested by fire; and so your faith, which is much more precious than gold, must also be tested, so that it may endure. Then you will receive praise and glory and honor on the Day when Jesus Christ is revealed.* GNT

This is all possible by changing the focus from "poor me" to "eternal blessings can come my way if I learn from my suffering." I suggest memorizing the next two verses to help create the kind of attitude designed to carry one through the trials of life. The burden is lightened when one trusts that God knows what is best and will work in concert with His saints who are suffering.

> *Romans 8:28 And we know that all things work together for good to those who love God, to those who are the called according to His purpose.* NKJV

The second scripture from which to gain strength acknowledges that human effort by itself is futile.

> *Philippians 4:11-13 I have learned to be content whatever the circumstances. I know what it is to be in need, and I know what it is to have plenty. I have learned the secret of being content in any and every situation, whether well fed or hungry, whether living in plenty or in want. I can do everything through him who gives me strength.* NIV

When anyone suffering realizes God will work all things for the good, and when he or she believes all things can be accomplished through Jesus Christ, the pressure is shifted from self-reliance to reliance upon God.

SUMMARY OF ACTIONS TO COPE WITH SUFFERING

Regardless of the reason for suffering, there are actions that can be taken in seeking relief.

1. Pray for strength and relief through God's grace and mercy.

When considering scripture dealing with suffering, several actions are possible to turn the tide. Those who believe God is sovereign are able to turn to prayer in times of need. Great examples of patriarchs such as Daniel and David stand as examples that God does hear the prayers of faithful followers. Job does a lot of speaking to the Lord, but it takes him a while to get his prayers fine-tuned. One's prayer should not be for God to change His mind and direction; rather, the prayer should be, "Lord, change me."

2. Rely on Jesus, our mediator.

A second action is to come to know the mediator and depend on Jesus for strength; the apostle Paul gained much strength in this way, and he advised his readers to do the same. We can do all things through Jesus Christ Who strengthens His disciples. Job is in an absolute quandary until Elihu arrives to identify the way to reach God.

3. Make the best of the circumstances.

Through the aid of prayer and strength from the Mediator, the one who is suffering needs to search for personal solutions. Though most want to know why they are suffering, the most important question to ask is "What do I need to do from where I am?" Other important questions can be probed: "How do I make the most out of my circumstances? What do I need to learn? How can I help others who are in need?" These questions are examples of forward thinking, opposed to dwelling on the past; forward thinking is generally productive in changing the focus from present miseries to hope in the future.

4. Strengthen faith in God.

During troubled times, it is imperative for suffering saints to work diligently to strengthen their faith. After all, if one believes in praying to the Father and relying on strength from the Mediator, he/she must not waver in belief that everything happening will somehow turn out right. Reading scripture to see the suffering of God's people will help in concluding, "I am not the only one to encounter pain." The more one understands the book of *Job*, the more he/she can identify with the suffering endured by a man who was blameless and upright.

The four actions above are not steps that necessarily come in sequence because each person walks through the "valley of death" in a different way. However, the four actions are all important in reaching the ideal of actually experiencing joy through suffering. These actions may alternate or even work in tandem with each other. Hopefully, praying, seeking strength from the Mediator, staying close to God's Word, and building faith will result in a feeling the world cannot explain.

STUDY GUIDE – Chapter 3

1. Discuss Job's wife's response after his body is covered with sores.

2. In what ways have you seen sin result in personal disaster?

3. How can we be sure Job's personal sin is not the cause of his disasters?

4. Why does God at times seem to administer group punishment?

5. Discuss ways the sins of the parents can affect their children.

6. Have you ever suffered because of your living a Christian life?

7. What is the difference in God's punishment and God's discipline?

8. How should one respond to personal tragedies?

CHAPTER 4

– MY FEELINGS ARE RUNNING WILD

Job experiences the stages of grief.

In 1969, Elisabeth Kubler-Ross authored a book, *On Death and Dying*, in which she introduced a grieving model with five-stages of grief: Denial, Anger, Bargaining, Depression, and Acceptance. Since 1969, other authors have tried to improve on the list by adding more and changing labels, but the stages identified by Kubler-Ross have stood the test of time. Throughout this chapter as the grief of Job is explored, these stages will be capitalized to highlight their presence in the process.

The groundwork for studies on grief was established millenniums earlier in the book of *Job*; the emotions and stages were not listed by name, but all five are easily identifiable. Kubler-Ross wrote that the stages are not steps in any particular order; the feelings and actions generated by the stages can come in multiples and can reappear at any time. I would suggest that Denial is almost universal as the first emotion after major losses, and Acceptance pretty well ends the process. However, grief is a process, and the middle three stages listed in her book may do a lot of shuffling before the ordeal ends. Furthermore, I have had years of helping others through the grief process, and I have seen various levels of Depression reappear in each of the stages.

JOB'S INITIAL REACTION OF DENIAL

When a major loss is experienced, most go through various forms of Denial. Some who are suffering say, "Everything's O.K.; I'm doing fine," when this is certainly not the case. One's early appearance of Acceptance of the tragedy is a sure sign of Denial. The reality of a major loss is too devastating to comprehend and process at the time, so Denial has the rule of the day. This initial response is a normal reaction to rationalize overwhelming emotions. To cope with the circumstances, Denial is used as a defense mechanism to mask the immediate shock. The suffering person is unable to voice his or her pain, and he/she hides from the facts. This temporary response carries the wounded through the first wave of pain.

Some who have made it through the process have explained their experience in terms such as: "I had no energy; my energy was drained." "I lost purpose in life for a period of time." "My faith wavered." These are all normal reactions to tremendous losses. While grief is a normal process, it is also adaptive when one learns from the situation and adapts and changes to meet the needs of the moment.

The subject of our study was the most prosperous man in the East, but he lost virtually everything around him in one day. All of this occurred when God turned Satan loose on Job with Satan's assurance that Job would break when things he treasured were lost. Imagine the stunned feeling Job had when all was lost in one day, as one servant after another approached him with bad news.

> *Job 1:13-19 One day when Job's sons and daughters were feasting and drinking wine at the oldest brother's house, a messenger came to Job and said, "The oxen were plowing and the donkeys were grazing nearby, and the Sabeans attacked and carried them off. They put the servants to the sword, and I am the only one who has escaped to tell you!"*
> *While he was still speaking, another messenger came and said, "The fire of God fell from the sky and burned up the sheep and the servants, and I am the only one who has escaped to tell you!"*
> *While he was still speaking, another messenger came and said, "The Chaldeans formed three raiding parties and swept down on your camels and carried them off. They put the servants to the sword, and I am the only one who has escaped to tell you!"*
> *While he was still speaking, yet another messenger came and said, "Your sons and daughters were feasting and drinking wine at the oldest brother's house, when suddenly a mighty*

wind swept in from the desert and struck the four corners of the house. It collapsed on them and they are dead, and I am the only one who has escaped to tell you! NIV

Imagine losing 7,000 sheep, 3,000 camels, 1,000 oxen (500 yoke of oxen), 500 donkeys, and all but 4 of a multitude of servants. Top this with the loss of 7 sons and 3 daughters, all in the same day. How is Job to respond to all these tragedies that occur in such a short time frame? DENIAL. Notice his quick, unrealistic response to the losses:

Job 1:20-21   Then Job arose and tore his robe and shaved his head, and he fell to the ground and worshiped. And he said: "Naked I came from my mother's womb, and naked shall I return there. The Lord gave, and the Lord has taken away; blessed be the name of the Lord." NKJV

The devastating events do not seem to budge Job at the time, so God sends Satan with more freedom to wreck Job's life. God is after something that will be identified later, but for now our focus is on Job's responses to the losses. God limits Satan from striking Job's person in round one, but in round two God's only limitation is for Satan not to take the life of Job. The Narrator does not tell us how much time transpires between the loss of Job's possessions and the loss of his health, but we are given the feeling that it is a short interval. Let's check out the description of his next shocker—loss of health.

Job 2:7-8   So Satan went forth from the presence of the Lord, and afflicted Job with loathsome sores from the sole of his foot to the crown of his head. And he took a potsherd with which to scrape himself, and sat among the ashes. RSV

Job's wife, upon observing her husband's intense suffering, urges him to let go of his integrity, to curse God and die. How does Job react to the misery coming from his sudden loss of health? DENIAL!

Job 2:10   But Job replied, "You talk like a foolish woman. Should we accept only good things from the hand of God and never anything bad?" So in all this, Job said nothing wrong. NLT

DEPRESSION SETS IN

Whenever any of us are going through what I call an "alligator pond," our suffering and losses seem to diminish when we read about the losses of Job. The severity of the debacles Job encounters perhaps explains the length of time he sits in stunned silence, a form of Depression. Generally one gets past Denial when reality begins removing the mask that all is fine; Depression can be defined as feelings of sadness, dejection, hopelessness, and gloom. Some Depression becomes so deep and serious that one attempts or accomplishes suicide. Depression is a serious state of being! Job's three friends, Eliphaz, Bildad, and Zophar arrive to sympathize with him and hopefully bring some comfort, but no one knows what to say to this man experiencing Depression.

> *Job 2:11-13   Three of Job's friends heard of all the trouble that had fallen on him. Each traveled from his own country — Eliphaz from Teman, Bildad from Shuhah, Zophar from Naamath — and went together to Job to keep him company and comfort him. When they first caught sight of him, they couldn't believe what they saw — they hardly recognized him! They cried out in lament, ripped their robes, and dumped dirt on their heads as a sign of their grief. Then they sat with him on the ground. Seven days and nights they sat there without saying a word. They could see how rotten he felt, how deeply he was suffering.* TM

The Narrator tells his readers the truth but does not explain every detail to answer interesting questions. 1) Do these men not drink water, eat food, or take care of bodily functions during this time? I have read claims that a person might be able to survive for 8 days without water and up to 14 days without food. This could possibly fit within the time frame, assuming they remain there throughout the conversations. Desert conditions such as arid land, heat, and wind reduce the ability to go for long periods without food or water; consequently, dehydration becomes a threat at some point. 2) Do they stay for seven consecutive days, or do they arrive to spend time on seven days at different times? Whatever the circumstances, the Narrator is simply letting us know that Job's Depression commingles with other stages throughout the ordeal.

JOB EXPRESSES ANGER OVER HIS CIRCUMSTANCES

The time consumed by Denial and Depression varies from person to person with Depression growing in the background, but reality is not pleasant, and the initial pain can re-emerge with vengeance. The intense emotion causes one to redirect the pain at inanimate objects, complete strangers, friends, or family. One of my former students expressed Anger at his deceased brother for dying in a motor cycle accident. I have heard patients scream at doctors and nurses who were unable to reverse medical conditions for them. Sometimes when a person flashes Anger at a loved one, he or she may feel Depression which, in turn, can lead to more Anger or to early stages of Acceptance. Anger is a normal reaction to major losses; the Anger may ultimately be thrown at God.

After several days of letting the losses soak in through the Denial and Depression stages, Job's pent up Anger flares. Job's friends must be stunned when the silence is broken and the pain deep within Job's mind comes boiling from his mouth! Job begins by cursing the day of his birth, but who made the day on which Job was born?

> *Job 3:1-7 In the end it was Job who broke the silence and cursed the day of his birth. This is what he said: "Perish the day on which I was born and the night that told of a boy conceived. May that day be darkness, may God on high have no thought for it, may no light shine on it. May murk and shadow dark as death claim it for their own, clouds hang over it, eclipse swoop down on it. See! Let obscurity seize on it, from the days of the year let it be excluded, into the reckoning of the months not find its way. And may that night be sterile, devoid of any cries of joy!"* NJB

Job wants to curse the day so badly, that his Anger leads him to long for others who could assist him in cursing the day.

During Bible times there were those who specialized in delivering curses. For example, in Numbers 22, Balak calls upon Balaam to curse Israel, and *Acts 13:8-9* describes a sorcerer named Elymas who may have delivered curses.

Whatever the situation, Job wants help in getting the task accomplished. He calls on those who "rouse Leviathan" (stir up trouble) to come to his aid. The word <u>Leviathan</u> refers to an alligator or Satan, reminding me of the "alligator ponds" to which I refer within this volume. Job's Anger is present in the following verse:

> *Job 3:8 "Let those curse it who curse the day, who are prepared to rouse Leviathan.* NASU

After seeking help from professional cursers and from those who are good at stirring up trouble, Job resumes the attack of the day of his birth because nothing intervened to stop his birth from occurring. Job's pain is so great that he expresses Anger over ever being alive in the first place. Death would be more pleasant. When reading the following passage, try to imagine the tone of voice coming from a man whose Anger has taken control:

> *Job 3:9-15 "May its morning stars become dark; may it wait for daylight in vain and not see the first rays of dawn, for it did not shut the doors of the womb on me to hide trouble from my eyes. Why did I not perish at birth, and die as I came from the womb? Why were there knees to receive me and breasts that I might be nursed? For now I would be lying down in peace; I would be asleep and at rest with kings and counselors of the earth, who built for themselves places now lying in ruins, with rulers who had gold, who filled their houses with silver."* NIV

Job next expands on the blessings of death. If the day of his birth had to exist, at least he could have been a stillborn child, joining others who were blessed by escaping their misery in death. It is very plain that Depression is present while Job's Anger is flashing over his present circumstances. Condemning life's state of affairs, Job is actually criticizing the way God has made the world and its creatures, and he is critical concerning God's method of ruling over mankind.

> *Job 3:16-22 "Why was I not buried like a stillborn child, like a baby who never lives to see the light? For in death the wicked cease from troubling, and the weary are at rest. Even prisoners at ease in death, with no guards to curse them. Rich and poor are there alike, and the slave is free*

from his master. Oh, why should light be given to the weary, and life to those in misery? They long for death, and it won't come. They search for death more eagerly than for hidden treasure. It is a blessed relief when they finally die, when they find the grave." NLT

After Job's Anger flashes against the day of his birth, he turns his Anger to life in general. Job's previous words have been aimed at God's decisions, but now Job makes it clear, beyond any doubt, that his complaint is against God.

Job 3:22-23 "They are not happy till they are dead and buried. God keeps their future hidden and hems them in on every side." GNT

JOB'S DEPRESSION RE-EMERGES

Throughout Job's initial bursts of Anger, he also experiences the state of Depression. As reality sets in following disaster, one's attention becomes centered on present circumstances. The emptiness caused by the losses draws the suffering party into deeper levels of grief. Will the suffering ever let up? Will it ever go away? Extreme Depression can lead to mental illness, but experiencing these feelings and thoughts is a normal reaction to a great loss. This is why Job longs for death, thinking perhaps, "Is there any point in going on alone? Why go on at all?" Depression is often viewed by those on the outside as being unnatural: a state to be fixed; they want the person to snap out of it. Not to experience Depression after a serious loss is unusual and unnatural. One can feel Job's Depression as the chapter ends.

Job 3:24-26 "For my groaning comes at the sight of my food, and my cries pour out like water. For what I fear comes upon me, and what I dread befalls me. I am not at ease, nor am I quiet, and I am not at rest, but turmoil comes. NAS

Job's Anger does not come to a screeching halt; but the reality of the moment allows the reader to look into the anguish in Job's soul. From this point of the story forward, Job's stages of Anger, Depression, and Bargaining will be seen in various forms until he begins moving into

41

Acceptance in *Job 40:3*. Job displays other flashes of Anger from chapter 6 through 31, and he will have many instances where he demands an audience with God as he dabbles with thoughts and expressions of Bargaining. Much more will be said about the stages of grief as this volume moves forward.

JOB WILL BE SEEKING TO BARGAIN WITH GOD THROUGHOUT THE BOOK

Job states his case for relief in many soliloquies pointed at confronting God face-to-face; however, he does not get an immediate audience. A classic case of Bargaining takes place in *Job 31:5-40* when Job explains how God should punish certain acts of wickedness of which, of course, Job claims to have no part. This is actually a plea for the Almighty to reconsider the actions He has aimed at Job.

WHEN GOD ARRIVES, JOB FINALLY HUMBLES HIMSELF IN ACCEPTANCE

After Job's blistering criticism of the Almighty and after Job encounters Elihu, God arrives to speak to Job out of a storm. Only after God questions Job's supremacy, abilities, and knowledge, does Job's awareness of God's power create the broken spirit and contrite heart necessary to bring about Acceptance. It takes Job a while to get there, but Job does persevere to make it through all five stages.

STUDY GUIDE – Chapter 4

1. Identify the stages of grief in Job's experience.

2. Which stage of grieving do you consider the most devastating?

3. Discuss Job's grief during the seven days he and his friends sit in silence.

4. Do you believe the seven days of grief are consecutive? Explain.

5. What implications are found in Job's cursing the day of his birth?

6. Is it alright to be angry with God?

7. Have you ever bargained with God?

8. What change of attitude leads to Job's acceptance of his circumstances?

CHAPTER 5

– WHY IS EVERYBODY PICKING ON ME?

Job's friends claim his sins have caused the calamities.

When tragedy strikes a family, friends generally respond in the best way they understand, but well-meaning people often have difficulty saying the right things. Paul wrote about the blessings brought by comforters who think before speaking.

> *2 Corinthians 1:3-4 What a wonderful God we have -- he is the Father of our Lord Jesus Christ, the source of every mercy, and the one who so wonderfully comforts and strengthens us in our hardships and trials. And why does he do this? So that when others are troubled, needing our sympathy and encouragement, we can pass on to them this same help and comfort God has given us.* LB

The Narrator relates that Job's friends had great intentions when they left their homes to assist in whatever way possible.

> *Job 2:11 Now when Job's three friends heard of all this adversity that had come upon him, each one came from his own place Eliphaz the Temanite, Bildad the Shuhite, and Zophar the Naamathite. For they had made an appointment together to come and mourn with him, and to comfort him.* NKJV

When one attempts to show sympathy and impart comfort with handy, over-used platitudes, these meaningless platitudes tend to work in the opposite direction. The person who is suffering isn't comforted hearing statements such as, "It could have been worse"; "God won't give you more than you can take"; "I understand how you feel." Victims are trying to sort through their losses, and worn-out phrases do not help change their focus.

So what should one do to help a friend or neighbor through a crisis? First and foremost, it is important to listen, listen, listen, and listen; just being there to lend an ear to a hurting friend can be of tremendous value. One should be patient and avoid interrupting the confused ramblings of the moment; angry, irrational comments may be heard, but this is a stage that should pass with time. When given an opportunity to speak, one should offer hope rather than false promises; this can be of assistance in changing the focus from the loss to hope in the future, a very important step to recovery.

How will Job's friends do in achieving their goal of mourning with him and comforting him? Their comments will fail in changing Job's focus to hope and recovery; in fact, their primary message condemns Job for sins that supposedly have brought about God's retribution. Before being too hard on the friends for their conclusions and accusations, keep in mind that many scriptures indicate blessings come to the upright, and tragedies seem to plague the ungodly. The concept that suffering is a consequence of God's retribution for sin is found in the passage below:

> *Psalms 18:25-26   To the faithful you show yourself faithful; to those with integrity you show integrity. To the pure you show yourself pure, but to the wicked you show yourself hostile. You rescue the humble, but you humiliate the proud.*   NLT

Ironically, we readers know Job is not being punished for his sins; we know this because the Narrator has already informed us that Job is a "blameless and upright man who fears God and shuns evil." A hint to what later will be shown to be a major factor in Job's suffering is found in the book of *Psalms*.

> *Psalms 18:27   You rescue the humble, but you humiliate the proud.*   NLT

If God punishes the haughty along with sinful beings, and if suffering comes from living in a sin infected world, how could Job's friends know the root cause of his suffering? To fully understand the direction taken by Eliphaz, Bildad, and Zophar, this chapter will focus primarily on their feeble attempts to explain suffering.

After seven days, Job's Depression moves him to break the silence. After Job's flashes of Anger in *Job 3:1-26*, the friends are ready to speak.

46

ELIPHAZ'S THREE SPEECHES

Understanding the steps one should take in rendering comfort, the reader can see that Eliphaz begins gently by referring to Job's help of others who have experienced tragedies. He explains that it is now time for Job to receive help from his friends. His relatively gentle comments to open the dialogue will soon change, but the opening few comments by Eliphaz are not too harsh.

> *Job 4:1-6 Then Eliphaz the Temanite replied: "If someone ventures a word with you, will you be impatient? But who can keep from speaking? Think how you have instructed many, how you have strengthened feeble hands. Your words have supported those who stumbled; you have strengthened faltering knees. But now trouble comes to you, and you are discouraged; it strikes you, and you are dismayed. Should not your piety be your confidence and your blameless ways your hope?"* NIV

Eliphaz should have paused at this point to see how Job responds; however, he continues his dialogue by intensifying the tension of the moment with a statement similar to "It could have been worse." He points out that Job did not perish in the losses suffered; then he notes that wicked actions bring God's retribution.

> *Job 4:7-11 "Think back now. Name a single case where someone righteous met with disaster. I have seen people plow fields of evil and plant wickedness like seed; now they harvest wickedness and evil. Like a storm, God destroys them in his anger. The wicked roar and growl like lions, but God silences them and breaks their teeth. Like lions with nothing to kill and eat, they die, and all their children are scattered."* GNT

Notice that Eliphaz illustrates the previous point by comparing powerful people, such as Job, to lions. He claims when rulers and princes of the earth become wicked and oppressive to their followers, God casts them down, breaks them to pieces, and destroys them. In his attempt to convince Job his wickedness has brought about disaster, Eliphaz claims his information came from a super-natural revelation.

Job 4:12-21 "Now a word was brought to me stealthily, and my ear received a whisper of it. Amid disquieting thoughts from the visions of the night, when deep sleep falls on men, dread came upon me, and trembling, and made all my bones shake. Then a spirit passed by my face; the hair of my flesh bristled up. It stood still, but I could not discern its appearance; a form was before my eyes; there was silence, then I heard a voice: 'Can mankind be just before God? Can a man be pure before his Maker? He puts no trust even in His servants; and against His angels He charges error. How much more those who dwell in houses of clay, whose foundation is in the dust, who are crushed before the moth! Between morning and evening they are broken in pieces; unobserved, they perish forever. Is not their tent-cord plucked up within them? They die, yet without wisdom.'" NAS

How could Job possibly counter a message received by Eliphaz from the spirit world? Having let Job know his message came from a supernatural source, he next turns to offering uninvited advice to his suffering friend. While Eliphaz could claim messages from the ethereal realm, he tells Job there is no point in his calling for help from the spirit world. Perhaps he is following up on an earlier point that angels have sinned and fallen; this being true, angels cannot help Job. His point may be that angels are under the direction of God; since God is punishing Job, there is no point in calling for their assistance. It is rather interesting that Job later pleads for a mediator, and the mediator theme will eventually take center stage when Elihu delivers his message. After this piece of advice for Job, Eliphaz makes a very disturbing statement to one who has just lost ten children in a destructive wind storm.

Job 5:3-7 "I have seen the foolish taking root, but suddenly the curse came on his house. Now his children have no safe place, and they are crushed before the judges, for no one takes up their cause. Their produce is taken by him who has no food, and their grain goes to the poor, and he who is in need of water gets it from their spring. For evil does not come out of the dust, or trouble out of the earth; But trouble is man's fate from birth, as the flames go up from the fire."   BBE

48

Whose household has suddenly been cursed? Whose children were uprooted from their place? Who has lost all his possessions to acts of God and to the Sabeans and Chaldeans? Job has lost all, and the words of Eliphaz do nothing but increase the wounds of Job and stir his Anger.

Good advice is given when Eliphaz encourages Job to make his appeal to God, but the words following the admonition are filled with barbs for the hurting man. In the following dialogue, Eliphaz tells Job that God helps the needy, so perhaps his losses will result in responses of mercy from God.

> *Job 5:8-16 "But if it were I, I would appeal to God; I would lay my cause before him. He performs wonders that cannot be fathomed, miracles that cannot be counted. He bestows rain on the earth; he sends water upon the countryside. The lowly he sets on high, and those who mourn are lifted to safety. He thwarts the plans of the crafty, so that their hands achieve no success. He catches the wise in their craftiness, and the schemes of the wily are swept away. Darkness comes upon them in the daytime; at noon they grope as in the night. He saves the needy from the sword in their mouth; he saves them from the clutches of the powerful. So the poor have hope, and injustice shuts its mouth."* NIV

Rather than the word <u>injustice</u> shuts its mouth, other versions use terms such as wicked, iniquity, unrighteousness, perverseness, and evil-doer. In other words, Eliphaz tells Job his mouth needs to remain shut because he firmly believes Job's hidden sins have brought about his dire circumstances.

Eliphaz ends his first soliloquy on a positive note, but future comments will indicate he does not fully understand the significance of his next statement.

> *Job 5:17 "Behold, how happy is the man whom God reproves, so do not despise the discipline of the Almighty."* NASU

Eliphaz hears Job curse the day of his birth and express his longing for relief from the grave. He even hears Job blame God for his misfortune; therefore, his response is understandable as he tries to get Job to accept misfortune and to focus on future blessings that could come from doing so. The writer of *Hebrews* must have been very familiar with Job's sufferings

49

and the outcome of his perseverance because *Hebrews 12:4-13* presents the same general message. Eliphaz tells Job to accept gracefully God's discipline.

After telling Job that blessings can come from suffering, he details the blessings God can bring about for those who accept His discipline.

> *Job 5:18-19 "For though he wounds, he also bandages. He strikes, but his hands also heal. He will rescue you again and again so that no evil can touch you. From six disasters he will rescue you; even in the seventh, he will keep you from evil."* NLT

The number 6, according to biblical symbol studies, is the number of humanity, mankind's having been created on day 6 of creation. Several Hebrew writings use the same technique of presenting a number, then adding one: *Amos 1:3-13, Amos 2:1-6,* and *Proverb 30:15-31.* Eliphaz adds one number to the 6 to reach the perfect number 7, indicating that God takes care of those who are righteous. The suggestion is that Job does not fit the category of righteousness. He then proceeds to detail the protection and care God affords to those who are strengthened through adversity:

> *Job 5:20-27 "In famine he will redeem you from death, and in war from the power of the sword. You shall be hidden from the scourge of the tongue, and shall not fear destruction when it comes. At destruction and famine you shall laugh, and shall not fear the wild animals of the earth. For you shall be in league with the stones of the field, and the wild animals shall be at peace with you. You shall know that your tent is safe, you shall inspect your fold and miss nothing. You shall know that your descendants will be many, and your offspring like the grass of the earth. You shall come to your grave in ripe old age, as a shock of grain comes up to the threshing floor in its season. See, we have searched this out; it is true. Hear, and know it for yourself."* NRS

Eliphaz began his soliloquy with sympathetic tact, but he turns on the steam as he ends. Read the above passage carefully and notice the specific references to the losses Job has just encountered. If God takes care of His people by keeping these kinds of things from happening, what does this say about Job? Eliphaz chastises Job by telling him to listen to the reproach and make the application to what has happened.

After Job rebuts the discourse of Zophar in *Job 12 - 14*, Eliphaz enters the fray for a second attempt to correct Job. He has listened to Job's explanation on the meaning of life and God's wisdom, so he attacks Job as being a "know it all." As you read his opening comments in *Job 15:1-13*, keep in mind the old saying, "It takes one to know one."

> *Job 15:1-6 Then Eliphaz the Temanite spoke and said: "Should a wise man answer with airy opinions, or puff himself up with wind? Should he argue in speech which does not avail, and in words which are to no profit? You in fact do away with piety, and you lessen devotion toward God, because your wickedness instructs your mouth, and you choose to speak like the crafty. Your own mouth condemns you, not I, your own lips refute you."* NJB

Eliphaz has insulted Job's speeches as being hot wind and words of no value, but he makes an even greater condemnation by asserting that Job's words are self-condemning, generated by his sin. In his first speech Eliphaz had claimed superior knowledge based on personal observation and supernatural revelation. Now he issues questions concerning Job's source of his knowledge:

> *Job 15:7-10 "Were you the first man to be born, or were you brought forth before the hills? Do you hear the secret counsel of God, limit wisdom to yourself? What do you know that we do not know? What do you understand that we do not? Both the gray-haired and the aged are among us, older than your father."* NAS

The previous verses leave the impression that Job must have been considered young, perhaps middle-aged. Eliphaz indicates the wisdom of age and experience is on the side of the three friends.

The Targum, an Aramaic translation dating sometime after about 500 BC, indicates the statement refers to Eliphaz himself and to his two friends as being the gray haired sages: Quoting the Targum: "Truly Eliphaz, who is hoary-headed and Bildad, the long-lived are with us, and Zophar, who is

51

older than your father." However, it may just be a claim that older people than they can support the friends' arguments. He claims that common knowledge passed down from former generations explains Job's demise. The next three verses have generated much discussion and disagreement:

> *Job 15:11-13 "Are God's consolations not enough for you, words spoken gently to you? Why has your heart carried you away, and why do your eyes flash, so that you vent your rage against God and pour out such words from your mouth?"* NIV

The Septuagint reads as follows: *"Thou hast been chastised less than thy sins deserve. Thou hast spoken with excessive haughtiness!"* This appears to be the most harsh, unacceptable statement anyone could make after Job's losses. After reading several opinions, the most logical explanation seems to be that Eliphaz is indicating God provided Job with three friends who arrive with gracious consolations; however, Job has been treating their attempts to help as being of no value because he has been rejecting every effort to comfort him. Eliphaz also makes reference to Job's nonverbal communication, speaking of his eyes "flashing" when he vents his Anger against God. Eliphaz has probably given an accurate description of Job's nonverbal signals of Anger.

In the next sequence of verses, Eliphaz renews and advances arguments to prove it is the wicked who receive punishment; therefore, Job must have secret sins that have warranted this kind of punishment. He begins by renewing an argument he previously has made in *Job 4:17-19* about the depraved nature of man:

> *Job 15:14-16 "What is man, that he could be pure, or one born of woman, that he could be righteous? If God places no trust in his holy ones, if even the heavens are not pure in his eyes, how much less man, who is vile and corrupt, who drinks up evil like water!"* NIV

Eliphaz really cuts to the chase when he begins a tirade based on personal observation and wisdom passed on to him by those who have observed life.

> *Job 15:17-24 "I will show you, hear me; and what I have seen I will declare (what wise men have told, and their*

fathers have not hidden, to whom alone the land was given, and no stranger passed among them). The wicked man writhes in pain all his days, through all the years that are laid up for the ruthless. Terrifying sounds are in his ears; in prosperity the destroyer will come upon him. He does not believe that he will return out of darkness, and he is destined for the sword. He wanders abroad for bread, saying, 'Where is it.' He knows that a day of darkness is ready at his hand; distress and anguish terrify him; they prevail against him, like a king prepared for battle." RSV

Why does a person suffer these things? Eliphaz paints a picture of Job's former speeches in which he criticizes God and heaps praises on himself The point Eliphaz made earlier concerning Job's bringing damage on himself with his own words is graphically described in the following claim that Job has positioned himself as God's enemy.

Job 15:24-26 "Trouble and anguish make him afraid; they overpower him, like a king ready for battle. For he stretches out his hand against God, and acts defiantly against the Almighty, running stubbornly against Him with his strong, embossed shield." NKJV

Eliphaz finishes his second soliloquy by describing the fate of the wicked. He may be describing Job in verse 27 when he refers to the wicked person's face being fat and his waist budging with flesh. The fate he describes is not a pleasant one. According to Eliphaz, Job is being paid in full for his sinful life, and he will not have children to carry on his name because his "branches will not flourish."

Job 15:27-35 "Though his face is covered with fat and his waist bulges with flesh, he will inhabit ruined towns and houses where no one lives, houses crumbling to rubble. He will no longer be rich and his wealth will not endure, nor will his possessions spread over the land. He will not escape the darkness; a flame will wither his shoots, and the breath of God's mouth will carry him away. Let him not deceive himself by trusting what is worthless, for he will get nothing in return. Before his time he will be paid in full, and his branches will not flourish. He will be like a vine stripped of its unripe grapes, like an olive tree shedding its blossoms. For the company of the godless will be barren, and fire will consume the tents of those who love bribes. They conceive trouble and give birth to evil; their womb fashions deceit." NIV

Eliphaz begins his third speech by claiming man means nothing to God; even a blameless man holds no special place. He has heard Job's claim of innocence and righteousness, so Eliphaz responds with a big "SO WHAT!"

Job 22:1-3 Then Eliphaz the Temanite replied: "Can a man be of benefit to God? Can even a wise man benefit him? What pleasure would it give the Almighty if you were righteous? What would he gain if your ways were blameless?" NIV

Eliphaz then changes gears to resume the thought that sin brings about punishment. The argument has not worked to this point, so Eliphaz resorts to listing the sins of Job. Since the Narrator has claimed Job was blameless and upright, this list of sins is an absolute fabrication.

Job 22:4-11 "Is it for your piety that he rebukes you and brings charges against you? Is not your wickedness great? Are not your sins endless? You demanded security from your brothers for no reason; you stripped men of their clothing, leaving them naked. You gave no water to the weary and you withheld food from the hungry, though you were a powerful man, owning land — an honored man, living on it. And you sent widows away empty-handed and broke the strength of the fatherless. That is why snares are all around you, why sudden peril terrifies you, why it is so dark you cannot see, and why a flood of water covers you." NIV

Job has not done any of these things; apparently Eliphaz has decided that claims of generic sin have not worked; therefore, he resorts to making up a few in hopes that something will stick. Eliphaz has heard Job claim God does not see things on earth, but Job had also claimed God is unaware of his impeccable life. In responding to this claim, Eliphaz assures Job that God does see through the clouds to reward the righteous and punish the wicked.

Job 22:12-18 "Is not God high in the heavens? See the highest stars, how lofty they are! Therefore you say, 'What does God know? Can he judge through the deep darkness? Thick clouds enwrap him, so that he does not see, and he walks on the dome of heaven.' Will you keep to the old way that the wicked have trod? They were snatched away before their time; their foundation was washed away by a flood. They said to God, 'Leave us alone,' and 'What can the Almighty do to us?' Yet he filled their houses with good things--but the plans of the wicked are repugnant to me." NRS

Eliphaz justifies the friends' attitudes by pointing out that many people rejoice when they see the downfall of the wicked. It is not joy over their sin, nor is it rejoicing over their misery; it is rejoicing that evil receives what it deserves. Eliphaz's subtle point seems to be that the friends are not rejoicing over Job's suffering; rather, they have been trying to help.

Job 22:19-20 "The righteous see it and are glad; the innocent laugh them to scorn, saying, 'Surely our adversaries are cut off, and what they left, the fire has consumed.'" NRS

Eliphaz ends his efforts by urging Job to repent from his wickedness, claiming that God will once again send blessings to him if he takes this step. God's blessings come to upright and blameless people, but Eliphaz informs Job that God will even deliver a sinner if he admits his wrongs and turns from his ways. While Job's friends were not exultant over Job's suffering, they would certainly rejoice if Job were to receive God's blessings after repenting.

Job 22:21-30 "Submit to God and be at peace with him; in this way prosperity will come to you. Accept instruction from his mouth and lay up his words in your heart. If you return to the Almighty, you will be restored: If you remove wickedness far from your tent and assign your nuggets to the dust, your gold of Ophir to the rocks in the ravines, then the Almighty will be your gold, the choicest silver for you. Surely then you will find delight in the Almighty and will lift up your face to God. You will pray to him, and he will hear

*you, and you will fulfill your vows. What you decide on
will be done, and light will shine on your ways. When
men are brought low and you say, 'Lift them up!' then he
will save the downcast. He will deliver even one who is
not innocent, who will be delivered through the cleanness
of your hands."* NIV

BILDAD'S THREE SPEECHES

As Job takes a breath after responding to Eliphaz's first speech, Bildad
jumps in with his perceptions; he is blunt and abrupt as he opens his
dialogue.

*Job 8:1-4 Then Bildad the Shuhite made answer and said,
"How long will you say these things, and how long will the
words of your mouth be like a strong wind? Does God give
wrong decisions? or is the Ruler of all not upright in his
judging? If your children have done evil against him, then
their punishment is from his hand."* BBE

We readers have been privileged to know wrong-doing has not caused
the suffering of Job. His maladies did not arrive because of law breaking,
and God was not bringing his vengeance through retribution. Bildad believes
retribution is the only possible explanation for Job's suffering, so he
indicates there is no possible explanation for these disasters other than Job's
and his family's sins. Having taken this position, Bildad urges Job to make
necessary corrections to receive the blessings God can provide.

*Job 8:5-7 "But if you will look to God and plead with the
Almighty, if you are pure and upright, even now he will
rouse himself on your behalf and restore you to your rightful
place. Your beginnings will seem humble, so prosperous
will your future be."* NIV

Eliphaz used a supernatural vision to bolster his claim to understanding
the events surrounding Job's disaster. Bildad urges Job to seek advice from
older, seasoned generations; their understanding of life will help Job
understand what is happening. After resorting to knowledge of the ancestors,
Bildad claims that common knowledge gained from observation of life

makes it plain that suffering comes from God's retribution when people sin. According to Bildad, if one can understand certain items of common knowledge, he/she should be able to see where, how, and why suffering occurs.

> *Job 8:8-13 "Put the question to our ancestors, study what they learned from their ancestors. For we're newcomers at this, with a lot to learn, and not too long to learn it. So why not let the ancients teach you, tell you what's what, instruct you in what they knew from experience? Can mighty pine trees grow tall without soil? Can luscious tomatoes flourish without water? Blossoming flowers look great before they're cut or picked, but without soil or water they wither more quickly than grass. That's what happens to all who forget God — all their hopes come to nothing."* TM

Having given the source of authority for his own arguments, he proceeds to say Job's reasoning and conclusions in answering Eliphaz have the strength of a spider web and the depth of a plant without deep roots.

> *Job 8:14-19 "What he trusts in is fragile; what he relies on is a spider's web. He leans on his web, but it gives way; he clings to it, but it does not hold. He is like a well-watered plant in the sunshine, spreading its shoots over the garden; it entwines its roots around a pile of rocks and looks for a place among the stones. But when it is torn from its spot, that place disowns it and says, 'I never saw you.' Surely its life withers away, and from the soil other plants grow."* NIV

Bildad then drops the axe by claiming Job's suffering clearly points to a guilty man. If Job were truly blameless, these devastating events would not have come his way. After making this statement, he offers Job a slight glimmer of hope that things will get better if he changes his ways. Bildad tries to leave no doubt that God does not attack the innocent!

> *Job 8:20-22 "Behold, God will not cast away the upright; neither will he take the hand of the wicked. Once more will he fill your mouth with laughter, and your lips with*

*rejoicing.   They that hate you shall be clothed with shame, and the tent of the wicked shall be no more." * NAS

The hair on the back of Bildad's neck is beginning to stand up as he listens to Job's attempts to defend himself, so he increases the onslaught in his second effort.

*Job 18:1-4 Then Bildad the Shuhite responded, "How long will you hunt for words? Show understanding and then we can talk. Why are we regarded as beasts, as stupid in your eyes? O you who tear yourself in your anger -- for your sake is the earth to be abandoned, or the rock to be moved from its place?" * NAS

After this blistering attack, Bildad returns to the same song, another verse, persistent throughout the friends' speeches. Reading the description of the suffering of the wicked and paying attention to his conclusion to the matter, the reader should have no question concerning Job's being the subject of the description.

*Job 18:5-21 "Surely the light of the wicked is put out, and the flame of their fire does not shine. The light is dark in their tent, and the lamp above them is put out. Their strong steps are shortened, and their own schemes throw them down. For they are thrust into a net by their own feet, and they walk into a pitfall. A trap seizes them by the heel; a snare lays hold of them. A rope is hid for them in the ground, a trap for them in the path. Terrors frighten them on every side, and chase them at their heels. Their strength is consumed by hunger, and calamity is ready for their stumbling. By disease their skin is consumed, the firstborn of Death consumes their limbs. They are torn from the tent in which they trusted, and are brought to the king of terrors. In their tents nothing remains; sulfur is scattered upon their habitations. Their roots dry up beneath, and their branches wither above. Their memory perishes from the earth, and they have no name in the street. They are thrust from light into darkness, and driven out of the world. They have no offspring or descendant among their people, and no survivor where they used to live. They of the west are appalled at *

*their fate, and horror seizes those of the east. Surely such
are the dwellings of the ungodly, such is the place of those
who do not know God."* NRS

Following Job's answer to Bildad, Zophar's second speech and Job's response, and Eliphaz's third speech, Job speaks again. In this discourse, Job complains about God's injustice. After hearing Job's complaint in *Job 23-24*, Bildad is ready to speak again in the shortest of the friends' speeches. Bildad may be on the way to understanding the reason for Job's disasters— Job's arrogance has run so wild that he has been critical of God Almighty. Bildad tries to explain the ways of God to Job in the shortest chapter of the book. This is Bildad's way of saying to Job, "You don't have a clue." His last statement in the following verses calls for Job to look at how unworthy he actually is:

*Job 25:1-6 Then Bildad the Shuhite replied: "Dominion
and awe belong to God; he establishes order in the heights
of heaven. Can his forces be numbered? Upon whom does
his light not rise? How then can a man be righteous before
God? How can one born of woman be pure? If even the
moon is not bright and the stars are not pure in his eyes,
how much less man, who is but a maggot — a son of man,
who is only a worm!"* NIV

Job follows Bildad's speech with the longest of all the speeches from *Job 25-31*, in which he instructs God regarding how judgment should take place.

ZOPHAR SHARES HIS INSIGHTS

Zophar has listened to speeches from Eliphaz and Bildad, and he has listened to Job's responses; having done so, Zophar is somewhat angry, so he cuts to the chase beginning with a direct attack on Job:

*Job 11:1-6 Then Zophar the Na'amathite answered:
"Should a multitude of words go unanswered, and a man full
of talk be vindicated? Should your babble silence men, and
when you mock, shall no one shame you? For you say, 'My
doctrine is pure, and I am clean in God's eyes.' But oh, that*

God would speak, and open his lips to you, and that he would tell you the secrets of wisdom! For he is manifold in understanding. Know then that God exacts of you less than your guilt deserves." RSV

It seems Job and his three friends are trying to outdo each other by showing their understanding of God's mighty works and reasons for His actions affecting the lives of humans. Zophar gives his insights on the subject:

Job 11:7-12 "Can you discover the depths of God? Can you discover the limits of the Almighty? They are high as the heavens; what can you do? Deeper than Sheol; what can you know? Its measure is longer than the earth and broader than the sea. If He passes by or shuts up, or calls an assembly, who can restrain Him? For He knows false men, and He sees iniquity without investigating. An idiot will become intelligent when the foal of a wild donkey is born a man." NASU

Zophar spends the remainder of his first speech calling for Job to repent from his ways in order to gain the blessings God has in store for the upright.

Job 11:13-14 "If you set your heart aright, you will stretch out your hands toward him. If iniquity is in your hand, put it far away, and let not wickedness dwell in your tents." RSV

It's rather clear that Zophar believes the cause of Job's disasters is sin; he instructs Job to make things right with God. He says if Job follows through to confess his sins before the Lord and turn his life around, blessings will definitely come.

Job 11:15-19 "Surely then you will lift up your face without blemish; you will be secure, and will not fear. You will forget your misery; you will remember it as waters that have passed away. And your life will be brighter than the noonday; its darkness will be like the morning. And you will have confidence, because there is hope; you will be protected {Or [you will look around]} and take your rest in safety. You will lie down, and no one will make you afraid; many will entreat your favor." NRS

Zophar claims that if Job does not follow his advice to receive the blessings mentioned above, he will be included among the wicked; he warns Job concerning what awaits him if he ignores the advice.

> *Job 11:20 "But the eyes of the wicked will fail, and escape will elude them; their hope will become a dying gasp."* NIV

Zophar's anger flashed in his first speech; he begins the second with renewed rage over the words of Job.

> *Job 20:1-3 Zophar of Naamath spoke next. He said: "My thoughts urge me to reply to this, and hence the impatience that grips me. I have put up with prating that outrages me and now my mind inspires me with an answer."* NJB

What do you suppose will be Zophar's answer to Job's suffering? Same song, still another verse, as he tries to convince Job it is only the wicked who suffer. He describes a generic scene in which a powerful man has his power ripped away. People look for the man they once knew, but that man is forever gone and will not return. Others are destined to clean up the mess the man left. Zophar is not that subtle in pointing to the status Job once held, and the loss of respect that now haunts him. He may be speaking about a generic person, but Job gets the point.

> *Job 20:4-10 "Do you not know, that since time began and human beings were set on the earth, the triumph of the wicked has always been brief, and the sinner's gladness has never lasted long? Towering to the sky he may have been, his head touching the clouds; but he vanishes, like a phantom, once for all, while those who used to see him, ask, 'Where is he?' Like a dream that leaves no trace he takes his flight, like a vision in the night he flies away. The eye accustomed to see him sees him no more, his home will never set eyes on him again. His sons will have to reimburse the poor and his children pay back his riches. His bones used to be full of youthful vigor: and there it lies, in the dust with him, now!"* NJB

Zophar's generic parable, aimed at Job, continues as he claims the powerful man's demise was caused by his sinful lifestyle. If one eats the fruits of sin, the aftereffects will always follow; he who plays with snakes ultimately suffers from their poisonous bite. These are the points Zophar makes in the following scripture:

> *Job 20:11-16 "Evil was sweet to his mouth, he would shelter it under his tongue; cultivating it carefully, he would let it linger on his palate. Such food goes bad in his belly, working inside him like the poison of a viper. Now he has to vomit up the wealth that he has swallowed, God makes him disgorge it. He used to suck vipers' venom, and the tongue of the adder kills him."* NJB

Zophar claims those who choose the path of wickedness suffer dire consequences; he ties wickedness to riches that cause a man to seek endless wealth. It's like the man who said, "I don't want all the land, just the land that touches mine." Zophar asserts that all the hoarding in the world will not be enough when God brings His wrath upon the wealthy man. Another point Zophar draws from his parable is that those who gather for themselves ultimately destroy those around them and will see their wealth and power destroyed in the process.

> *Job 20:17-22 "No more will he know the streams of oil or the torrents of honey and cream. When he gives back his winnings, his cheerfulness will fade, and the satisfied air he had when business was thriving. Since he once destroyed the huts of the poor, plundering houses instead of building them up, since his avarice could never be satisfied, now all his hoarding will not save him; since nothing could escape his greed, his prosperity will not last. When he has everything he needs, want will seize him, and misery will light on him with all its force."* NJB

Zophar concludes his parable by explaining that God's fury brings about the collapse of the rich man's empire. If God's right hand doesn't get him, the left one will because God brings all his powers against such wicked people. Could Job miss the underlying message of Zophar's pointed analogy of power, abuse of power, loss of power, and vengeance of God?

> *Job 20:23-29 "When the wicked fill their stomachs, God will send his burning anger against them, and blows of*

punishment will fall on them like rain. The wicked may run away from an iron weapon, but a bronze arrow will stab them. They will pull the arrows out of their backs and pull the points out of their livers. Terrors will come over them; total darkness waits for their treasure. A fire not fanned by people will destroy them and burn up what is left of their tents. The heavens will show their guilt, and the earth will rise up against them. A flood will carry their houses away, swept away on the day of God's anger. This is what God plans for evil people; this is what he has decided they will receive." NCV

Perhaps the friends thought Job's hearing of the same message enough times, would somehow help turn his life around. Don't forget that the Narrator has already described Job as blameless and upright, a man who feared God. Job cannot be described accurately as an ungodly man, but we can know for a fact that God has a reason for bringing about Job's suffering. Just as one would suspect, Job doesn't buy into his friends' analysis, regardless of the number of times they repeat the message. The next three chapters will explore Job's responses to the eight speeches delivered by his friends.

STUDY GUIDE – Chapter 5

1. Have you ever wanted to help someone suffering but didn't know what to say?

2. Discuss the importance of listening to one who is suffering.

3. How does Eliphaz try to create credibility and strengthen his case?

4. Evaluate Eliphaz's good and bad points.

5. How does Bildad try to support his arguments?

6. How effective is Bildad in approaching a suffering man?

7. How effective is Zophar's parable?

8. Why were the three friends unable to get anywhere with Job?

CHAPTER 6

– WHICH WAY IS UP?

Job wavers between depression and hope.

When one is coping with grief, Depression is present in the stages of Denial and Anger; as Depression runs its course, it competes with hope. Have you ever suffered a loss and found yourself in despair one moment and looking for the light at the end of the tunnel the next? Depression focuses on past losses, while hope focuses on future relief. The more one's thoughts center on the future, the fewer thoughts of Depression invade the mind. Depression is present because of what is perceived as a "hopeless situation"; if something is hopeless, the opposite is hope.

One of my friends had a wise saying to share when a parent was overly concerned about a child who was drifting into troubled waters. She would ask, "Is he or she still breathing?" If the answer was "Yes," the next statement was, "Then there is still hope." This is the thought expressed by the Psalmist:

> *Psalms 118:18 The LORD has disciplined me severely, but He has not given me over to death.* NAS

If there is still life, God is granting time for lessons to be learned and for circumstances to be reversed. Scripture teaches that difficult times and suffering has its positive side as well. If this truth can be grasped, the possibility of hope's overcoming Depression is much greater. In explaining this awesome principle, the writer of *Hebrews* quotes *Proverbs 3:11-12*.

> *Hebrews 12:4-11 In your struggle against sin, you have not yet resisted to the point of shedding your blood. And you have forgotten that word of encouragement that addresses you as sons: "My son, do not make light of the Lord's discipline, and do not lose heart when he rebukes you,*

because the Lord disciplines those he loves, and he punishes everyone he accepts as a son." Endure hardship as discipline; God is treating you as sons. For what son is not disciplined by his father? If you are not disciplined (and everyone undergoes discipline), then you are illegitimate children and not true sons. Moreover, we have all had human fathers who disciplined us and we respected them for it. How much more should we submit to the Father of our spirits and live! Our fathers disciplined us for a little while as they thought best; but God disciplines us for our good, that we may share in his holiness. No discipline seems pleasant at the time, but painful. Later on, however, it produces a harvest of righteousness and peace for those who have been trained by it. NIV

The truth found in the above passage can be found in a real world scenario when one reads the book of *Job*. Job does not find the discipline pleasant, and he voices his disapproval and exhibits signs of Depression throughout the suffering. However, Job finally rises above the trauma because of his faith in God and his contact with God's mediator, Elihu. The apostle Paul probably relied on insights gained from Job's experiences; Paul explained what he had learned about persevering through all types of adverse situations:

Philippians 4:12-13   I know what it is to have little, and I know what it is to have plenty. In any and all circumstances I have learned the secret of being content in any and every situation, whether well-fed and of going hungry, of having plenty and of being in need. I can do all things through him who strengthens me. NRS

As the speeches of Job are examined, it becomes clear that Depression is often overwhelming to the point of his longing to die. If feelings of this nature last for long periods, suicide often becomes the solution for relief. Job, however, expresses hope for God's relief to come, and he maintains his trust in the Almighty.

JOB'S EMOTIONAL STATE DESCRIBED AFTER ELIPHAZ'S SPEECH

Job Wavers between depression and hope.

If Job's friends had listened carefully to him, surely they would have realized his irrational comments were coming from a distressed heart. After Eliphaz's first speech, Job does a good job explaining the feeling of pain:

> *Job 6:1-4 "If my sadness could be weighed and my troubles be put on the scales, they would be heavier than all the sands of the sea. That is why I spoke so rashly. For the Almighty has struck me down with his arrows. He has sent his poisoned arrows deep within my spirit. All God's terrors are arrayed against me."* NLT

Job makes an interesting comparison of himself to a wild donkey's braying when no food can be found. He believes he should be given the same right to "bray" because of the great losses he has suffered. Perhaps he understands that his friends are comparing his stubborn nature to that of a donkey. The three friends can understand the donkey, so Job wonders why they cannot understand him.

> *Job 6:5-7 "Don't I have a right to complain? Wild donkeys bray when they find no green grass, and oxen low when they have no food. People complain when there is no salt in their food. And how tasteless is the uncooked white of an egg! My appetite disappears when I look at it; I gag at the thought of eating it!"* NLT

Because his Depression is weighing heavily on his shoulders, Job returns to the theme used when he spoke for the first time after his calamities, "I wish I could die!"

> *Job 6:8 "Oh, that I might have my request, that God would grant my hope. I wish he would crush me. I wish he would reach out his hand and kill me.* NLT

Job continues expressing his desire to die, and in this next sequence of verses, he reveals more about his despair and questions whether there is any reason for hope. Job's strength is sapped, and he is at the end of his rope.

The struggle between Depression and hope could not be clearer than it is in the following verses:

> *Job 6:11-14 "What strength do I have, that I should still hope? What prospects, that I should be patient? Do I have the strength of stone? Is my flesh bronze? Do I have any power to help myself, now that success has been driven from me? A despairing man should have the devotion of his friends, even though he forsakes the fear of the Almighty."* NIV

Job has many things to say directed at his friends and directed at God, but he does not complete this speech without more expressions concerning his feelings of Depression. He describes the plight of mankind, noting that mankind is on earth for just a short time that is filled with difficulties.

> *Job 7:1-3 "Is not man forced to labor on earth, and are not his days like the days of a hired man? As a slave who pants for the shade, and as a hired man who eagerly waits for his wages, so am I allotted months of vanity, and nights of trouble are appointed me."* NASU

Job's suffering is magnified by his inability to sleep; he describes lying in bed, tossing and turning while waiting for morning to come. These kinds of nights are the longest a person ever experiences. If one goes through several sleepless nights, Depression becomes deeper. Job tells of his sleepless nights in the next sequence:

> *Job 7:3-4 "So am I allotted months of vanity, and nights of trouble are appointed me. When I lie down I say, 'When shall I arise?' But the night continues, and I am continually tossing until dawn."* NASU

Job's body has been covered with sores, and he has scraped himself with stones to deal with the pain. He describes his physical condition and once again expresses that his days will end without hope. At this point in Job's dialogues, it appears that Depression is winning the struggle against hope.

Job 7:5-6 "My flesh is clothed with worms and a crust of dirt. My skin hardens and runs. My days are swifter than a weaver's shuttle, and come to an end without hope." NASU

While talking to his friends, Job often directs comments to God concerning his agony. Job compares himself to a cloud that appears for a short time and then is gone; he will soon die and exist no more. Job's feeling of hopelessness leads him to say he has nothing to lose by expressing his anguish to the Lord. In later speeches, Job expresses hope of eternal life, but at this point his despair continues to lead him to doubt. Doubt creates Depression; hope finds its strength in trust. After Eliphaz's speech, Job's words reveal despair with no sign of hope.

Job 7:7-11 "Remember that my life is but breath; my eye will not again see good. The eye of him who sees me will behold me no longer; Your eyes will be on me, but I will not be. When a cloud vanishes, it is gone, so he who goes down to Sheol does not come up. He will not return again to his house, nor will his place know him anymore. Therefore I will not restrain my mouth; I will speak in the anguish of my spirit, I will complain in the bitterness of my soul." NASU

JOB'S COMMENTS AFTER BILDAD'S SPEECH

A mixture of despair and hope is found within Job's rejoinder to Bildad's speech. Job compares his misery to the pain endured by a long-distance runner. In Job's era, messages were carried by runners, but his pain is much swifter, greater than that endured by the runners. He also compares his quandary to "skiffs of reed," paper weight boats that move swiftly in the water. In his commentary, Adam Clarke explains this as light weight vessels used by pirates. It is possible that Job is saying that his circumstance is much like pirates stripping him of his property and swiftly making their escape with the booty. In the following passage, Job further compares his losses to a bird of prey swooping down to devour his family and possessions:

Job 9:25-26 "My days are swifter than a runner, they flee away; they see no happiness; They shoot by like skiffs of reed, like an eagle swooping upon its prey." NJB

69

Job tries to change his focus to happy images, but his thoughts of anguish draw him back to the conclusion that all is hopeless. He once again addresses God, saying there is nothing he can do to remedy the situation. Because Job is relying on his own abilities and efforts to alleviate pain, he believes relief is hopeless. Depression is having its day.

> *Job 9:27-31 "If I say: 'I will forget my complaining; I will lay aside my sadness and be of good cheer.' Then I am in dread of all my pains; I know that you will not hold me innocent. If I must be accounted guilty, why then should I strive in vain? If I should wash myself with snow and cleanse my hands with lye, yet you would plunge me in the ditch, so that my garments would abhor me."* NJB

Although Depression is controlling the mind of Job, he continues contemplating a way to find relief. Once he concludes there is nothing he can do, Job identifies the problem—God's power. However, Job then expresses hope and desire for a mediator to step in and plead his case:

> *Job 9:32-35 "God is not a mortal like me, so I cannot argue with him or take him to trial. If only there were a mediator between us, someone who could bring us together. The mediator could make God stop beating me, and I would no longer live in terror of his punishment. Then I could speak to him without fear, but I cannot do that in my own strength."* NLT

It appears that Job may be finding a ray of hope, but his mood once again sinks into melancholy:

> *Job 10:1 "I am disgusted with my life. Let me complain freely. My bitter soul must complain."* NLT

JOB SEEKS HOPE AFTER ZOPHAR'S SPEECH

Job appears to be on the way toward healing when he speaks of his desire for a mediator; however, in response to Zophar's speech, he returns to his mistaken belief that his only hope is in his own righteousness. Because he is convinced of his own righteousness, Job believes he will be vindicated when God hears his case.

Job 13:15-19 "Though He slay me, I will hope in Him. Nevertheless I will argue my ways before Him. This also will be my salvation, for a godless man may not come before His presence. Listen carefully to my speech, and let my declaration fill your ears. Behold now, I have prepared my case; I know that I will be vindicated. Who will contend with me? For then I would be silent and die." NASU

In the passage above, Job's arrogance hits its peak as he develops his case for presentation to God. How haughty to think one can stand before God and challenge the Almighty! Job's Depression runs amuck when he puts his trust in his own abilities and power; Job's pride separates him from the real solution—trust in God. When God appears after Job's encounter with the mediator, God will address Job's arrogance. When reading the following passage, keep in mind that this is God's message to Job:

Job 40:8-14 "Would you discredit my justice? Would you condemn me to justify yourself? Do you have an arm like God's, and can your voice thunder like his? Then adorn yourself with glory and splendor, and clothe yourself in honor and majesty. Unleash the fury of your wrath, look at every proud man and bring him low, look at every proud man and humble him, crush the wicked where they stand. Bury them all in the dust together; shroud their faces in the grave. Then I myself will admit to you that your own right hand can save you." NIV

If man's hope is in himself and in his own righteousness, there is no real hope; however, for the moment, this is Job's misdirected attempt to fight Depression. As Job continues wavering between hope and despair, notice how he compares man's life to a flower and to a shadow; neither one stays around long. This is the way Job views his own life.

Job 14:1-2 "Man born of woman is short-lived and full of trouble, like a flower that springs up and fades, swift as a shadow that does not abide." NAB

Job refers to hope once more, but this time he is referring to a tree that is cut down; it may appear that the tree is totally removed, but there is still hope that it will return. Years ago I transplanted a mulberry tree from our front

71

yard to the back yard. The tree looked absolutely dead the remainder of the year, but then it sprouted a leaf at the base that grew into a huge tree. In the passage below, Job is distressed because there is hope for a tree that looks dead, but there is no hope for him:

> *Job 14:7-9 "For a tree there is hope, if it be cut down, that it will sprout again and that its tender shoots will not cease. Even though its root grow old in the earth, and its stump die in the dust, yet at the first whiff of water it may flourish again and put forth branches like a young plant."* NAB

Man's fate is contrasted with that of a tree as Job continues his dialogue; Job seems to believe in life after death in the passage below, but he is distraught over the advantage trees hold over humans. Job indicates he would prefer to be in the grave (Sheol) as he waits for his day in God's court:

> *Job 14:10-15 "But mortals die, and are laid low; humans expire, and where are they? As waters fail from a lake, and a river wastes away and dries up, so mortals lie down and do not rise again; until the heavens are no more, they will not awake or be roused out of their sleep. O that you would hide me in Sheol, that you would conceal me until your wrath is past, that you would appoint me a set time, and remember me!"* NRS

One undeniable factor of Job's Depression stems from doubts arising over the after-life. Notice in the following passage that Job questions whether there is a resurrection of the dead. After expressing some doubt, hope seems to emerge once more as he indicates belief that he will one day see God.

> *Job 14:14-15 "If mortals die, will they live again? All the days of my service I would wait until my release should come. You would call, and I would answer you; you would long for the work of your hands."* NRS

Job is confident that his righteousness will clear him of any wrongdoing; he seems to think that in the after-life all will be made right. Earlier he claimed to have no sin, but now he expresses some hope that in the long run God will cover over any sin he has on his record.

Job 14:16-17 "Then you will watch every step I take, but you will not keep track of my sins. You will forgive them and put them away; you will wipe out all the wrongs I have done." GNT

Any hope Job seems to be developing disappears as Job returns to his message of gloom and despair. If Job's situation is absolutely hopeless, whose fault is it? Is it a lack of faith and trust on Job's part, or can Job find a way to blame his lack of hope on another source? Job not only blames God as being the source of his Depression, but he also accuses God of destroying hope:

Job 14:18-22 "But as a mountain erodes and crumbles and as a rock is moved from its place, as water wears away stones and torrents wash away the soil, so you destroy man's hope. You overpower him once for all, and he is gone; you change his countenance and send him away. If his sons are honored, he does not know it; if they are brought low, he does not see it. He feels but the pain of his own body and mourns only for himself." NIV

JOB'S STRUGGLE AFTER ELIPHAZ'S SECOND SPEECH

Eliphaz completes his second attempt to set the record straight, and Job responds with an Anger flash at his friends before turning once again to descriptions of hopelessness. There is nothing Job can do that can possibly bring about his relief.

Job 16:6-7 "When I speak up, I feel no better; if I say nothing, that doesn't help either. I feel worn down. God, you have wasted me totally — me and my family!" TM

Despite his failed efforts, Job still holds hope that his pain and penance will garner God's attention and bring relief his way. He describes some of the actions that make his sorrow rather evident. However, his arrogance jumps out once more at the end of this sequence when he describes his purity.

Job 16:15-17 "I sewed myself a shroud and wore it like a shirt; I lay face down in the dirt. Now my face is blotched

red from weeping; look at the dark shadows under my eyes, even though I've never hurt a soul and my prayers are sincere!" TM

Job's comments below indicate that Depression has not taken complete control because he makes a tremendously strong statement of hope. He makes another reference concerning his mediator/intercessor; his trust in God has wavered in previous comments, but it is still present in some small degree. Most of Job's thoughts about solutions have revolved around his capabilities, but in the sequence below, he recognizes the need for someone to plead for him.

> *Job 16:18-21 "O earth, do not cover my blood; may my cry never be laid to rest! Even now my witness is in heaven; my advocate is on high. My intercessor is my friend as my eyes pour out tears to God; on behalf of a man he pleads with God as a man pleads for his friend."* NIV

Readers are pleased to hear Job's statement of faith, but about the time it appears he is close to Acceptance, his wavering between Depression and hope returns, and he voices his despair below:

> *Job 16:22-17:2 "Only a few years will pass before I go on the journey of no return. My spirit is broken, my days are cut short, the grave awaits me. Surely mockers surround me; my eyes must dwell on their hostility."* NIV

Job's distraught spirit can further be witnessed in the following verses as he describes his feelings and his awareness of his gaunt appearance.

> *Job 17:7 "My eye has also grown dim because of grief, and all my members are as a shadow."* NAS

> *Job 17:11 "My days are past, my plans are torn apart, even the wishes of my heart."* NAS

Job's speech ends with a despairing statement of hopelessness. Job is convinced there will be no relief while he is alive. His hope is going to die with him.

> *Job 17:14-16 "If I call to the pit, 'You are my father'; to the worm, 'my mother and my sister'; where now is my hope?*

And who regards my hope? Will it go down with me to Sheol? Shall we together go down into the dust?" NAS

DESPAIR AND HOPE AFTER BILDAD'S SECOND SPEECH

Loss of prestige and damaged image can become huge in the minds of those who fall from their pedestals. Job is not only distraught because he has lost health and wealth; the strongest catalyst causing his Depression may be the new way in which he is viewed by those who once bowed in his presence.

> *Job 19:15-20 "Those who live in my house and my maids consider me a stranger. I am a foreigner in their sight. I call to my servant, but he does not answer, I have to implore him with my mouth. My breath is offensive to my wife, and I am loathsome to my own brothers. Even young children despise me; I rise up and they speak against me. All my associates abhor me, and those I love have turned against me. My bone clings to my skin and my flesh, and I have escaped only by the skin of my teeth."* NAS

A real piece of irony comes next as Job expresses the desire to have the words of his misery recorded. Printing presses were centuries away from existence, but methods of writing obviously existed for this statement to have been made. Scrolls have existed for millenniums, and Job hopes someone might write about his sufferings. It is amazing that modern readers have access to the story of his suffering and the misery through which he persevered because someone took the time and effort to help future generations make it through the grieving process.

> *Job 19:23-24 "How I wish my words were written down, written on a scroll. I wish they were carved with an iron pen into lead, or carved into stone forever."* NCV

Depression is running high at this point in Job's dialogue, but hope will have more to say; Job still maintains belief in God and hope in a Redeemer. Much conjecture has taken place concerning the following passage. Some believe it refers to Job's belief and hope that his circumstances will be reversed. Others believe the Spirit moved Job at this time to speak prophetically about the resurrection of all mankind. There is no definitive answer to this discussion, but let it suffice for basic understanding to note that Job's hope is still present.

> *Job 19:25-27* *"For I know that my Redeemer lives, and at the last he will stand upon the earth. And after my skin has been thus destroyed, yet in my flesh I shall see God, whom I shall see for myself, and my eyes shall behold, and not another. My heart faints within me!"* ESV

JOB'S COMMENTS AFTER ZOPHAR SPEAKS

Depression is certainly present throughout Job's speech in response to Zophar; however, he makes no descriptions of the suffering he is experiencing, and he makes no comments indicating the hope he has for redemption. Rather, he spends his time pointing out that the wicked are not punished for their sins; he sees this as injustice. After all, Job has walked the line, and he believes he is in the "alligator pond" for no just reason.

JOB'S RESPONSE TO ELIPHAZ'S THIRD SPEECH

Job opens by justifying his rash comments, describing the misery he is experiencing in the following verse:

> *Job 29:2* *"Today also my complaint is bitter; his hand is heavy despite my groaning."* NRS

Following this opening comment, Job once again describes the hope that his own righteousness will pull him through. If he can only find God to get the hearing he deserves, God will surely see Job's point and alleviate his burdens. He develops this thought in *Job 29:3-17*; Job is convinced his righteousness will be his redemption.

Job's Depression and Anger drive him to examine the activities of evil people, and he demands that God has been unjust. Job claims that God allows these atrocities to take place before issuing the following challenge to his three friends:

Job 24:25 "Now if it is not so, who will prove me a liar, and make my speech worth nothing?" NKJV

JOB RESPONDS TO BILDAD'S THIRD SPEECH

Bildad delivers the shortest speech in the debate over suffering; this is followed by the longest speech in the debate, delivered by Job, covering 6 chapters and 158 verses. In making the count, I did not include statements such as "Job said," "Job continued"; the only ones counted involved the actual words of Job. In this long tirade, Job expresses nothing in the way of hope. His total speeches cover 501 verses; in these he justifies himself, criticizes God, condemns his friends, and reveals his confused emotions as he vacillates between Depression and hope. As he nears the end of his comments, Job's Depression dominates his thoughts.

Once more Job is distraught over his loss of status, and he blames all his maladies on the Lord. During these days of coping with Anger and Depression, he is unable to accept any responsibility for his circumstances. In his mind the suffering is an unjust act of God. No wonder Job describes the following feelings of despair:

> *Job 30:9-15 "And now I have become their taunt, I have even become a byword to them. They abhor me and stand aloof from me, and they do not refrain from spitting at my face. Because He has loosed His bowstring and afflicted me, they have cast off the bridle before me. On the right hand their brood arises; they thrust aside my feet and build up against me their ways of destruction. They break up my path, they profit from my destruction; no one restrains them. As through a wide breach they come, amid the tempest they roll on. Terrors are turned against me; they pursue my honor as the wind, and my prosperity has passed away like a cloud. NASU*

Job has presented many colorful phrases to describe his misery; one would have a difficult time reading the passage below without feeling the pain of Job.

Job 30:16-19 "And now my soul is poured out within me; days of affliction have taken hold of me. The night racks my bones, and the pain that gnaws me takes no rest. With great force my garment is disfigured; it binds me about like the collar of my tunic. God has cast me into the mire and I have become like dust and ashes." ESV

In the next few verses as Job cries out to God for justice, he doesn't see the need for mercy since he "believes he" is in the right. He is upset for the treatment and criticizes God for injuries inflicted on such a righteous person. His Anger comes between statements of Depression without hope. In the passage below, Job continues describing the misery he feels:

Job 30:27-31 "My stomach's in a constant churning, never settles down. Each day confronts me with more suffering. I walk under a black cloud. The sun is gone. I stand in the congregation and protest. I howl with the jackals, I hoot with the owls. I'm black and blue all over, burning up with fever. My fiddle plays nothing but the blues; my mouth harp wails laments." TM

At this point, Job appears to be a long way from reaching Acceptance, but all will begin to change once Job listens to the mediator and begins to recognize the difference between God and himself. It is possible to take comfort when disasters come our way, just knowing that God understands when we go through the stages of grief on the way to reaching the peace of Acceptance. Job perseveres through it all, and we can also persevere through Jesus, our Mediator, who gives us strength.

Philippians 4:11-13 I have learned to be content whatever the circumstances. I know what it is to be in need, and I know what it is to have plenty. I have learned the secret of being content in any and every situation, whether well fed or hungry, whether living in plenty or in want. I can do all this through him who gives me strength TNIV

Job's perseverance has given courage to many such as the apostle Paul, and the same principle continues to be effective today when those who are suffering seek God in the midst of pain.

STUDY GUIDE – Chapter 6

1. Discuss the effects of backward thinking vs. forward thinking.

2. What thoughts of Job best express his Depression?

3. What does Job see as the reason for his Depression?

4. What do you see as the reason for Job's Depression?

5. What is significant about Job's hope for a mediator?

6. Why is hope in self built on false premises?

7. Discuss Job's thoughts over resurrection and the after-life.

8. How was Job's Depression brought under control?

CHAPTER 7

– ANYTHING YOU CAN DO, I CAN DO BETTER!

Job criticizes his friends and praises himself.

Eliphaz, Bildad, and Zophar are kind enough to leave their homes and sit in silence with Job for seven days, mourning with him over his losses. When Job breaks the silence with Anger over his birth and his losses, the three friends respond. They are unrelenting during eight speeches in an effort to convince Job of the need to repent because they believe his secret sins have led to the collapse of his empire.

Granted, the three friends arrive at the wrong conclusion for Job's suffering, but let's give them credit for being interested in his recovery from multi-tragedies that have struck his family, possessions, and personal health. In *Job 1 - 2,* the Narrator informs readers that Job was a blameless and upright man who feared God and shunned evil. Job knows he has lived a cut above those around him, and he believes his health and wealth stem from righteous living. Job's belief in this principle causes him to dwell in silent Denial for a while, but the same understanding later drives his Anger over the disasters that have turned his life upside down. If health and wealth are rewards for purity, then why has he, a blameless and upright man, lost it all?

Anyone seeking to follow God's plan for his or her life has two spirits at work within; the physical spirit seeks things of the world, and the Spirit of God seeks the righteous path. The apostle Paul describes this dual nature in the following passage:

> *Romans 8:5-8 Those who live according to the sinful nature have their minds set on what that nature desires; but those who live in accordance with the Spirit have their minds set on what the Spirit desires. The mind of sinful man is death, but the mind controlled by the Spirit is life and peace; the*

sinful mind is hostile to God. It does not submit to God's
law, nor can it do so. Those controlled by the sinful nature
cannot please God. NIV

Since the two are by nature opposed to each other, one of the two spirits must ultimately give way to the other; God's desire for the human spirit to submit is expressed in the following passage:

Psalms 51:17 The sacrifice you desire is a broken spirit. You
will not reject a broken and repentant heart, O God. NLT

David is said to be "a man after God's own heart,' but David made many mistakes in life when he allowed his human spirit to take charge. David's spirit had to be broken before God's Spirit could work within him.

There is no question that Job has lived an upright life, but Job is proud of his blameless life. Something must happen to break his love of self, a common malady called narcissism, which destroys those possessed by arrogance. The Narrator does not tell us how long Job has known his friends, but Job believes he is superior; consequently, his Anger flashes as he rejects his friends' analysis of God's retribution, and his arrogance emerges as he praises himself.

JOB'S SECOND SPEECH

Job's Anger, mixed with Depression, is expressed after Eliphaz completes his first attempt to correct Job. Job repeats his preference for death over the suffering he is enduring. He is convinced eternal blessings await him upon death; after all, he has not broken faith with God. Since death would end the suffering, Job once again longs for death and insists he has done no wrong:

Job 6:8-10 "Oh, that I might have my request, that God
would grant what I hope for, that God would be willing to
crush me, to let loose his hand and cut me off! Then I would
still have this consolation — my joy in unrelenting pain —
that I had not denied the words of the Holy One." NIV

Jobs' friends sit in silence for seven days without offering any verbal assistance, so Job compares them to a dried up stream that disappoints those hoping to find water. He blames confusion and fear for their ineptness to comfort him properly. Job does not appreciate the comments offered by Eliphaz, so he attacks the messenger:

> *Job 6:14-21 "To him who is afflicted, kindness should be shown by his friend, even though he forsakes the fear of the Almighty. My brothers have dealt deceitfully like a brook, like the streams of the brooks that pass away, which are dark because of the ice, and into which the snow vanishes. When it is warm, they cease to flow; when it is hot, they vanish from their place. The paths of their way turn aside, they go nowhere and perish. The caravans of Tema look, the travelers of Sheba hope for them. They are disappointed because they were confident; they come there and are confused. For now you are nothing, you see terror and are afraid."* NKJV

Job's self-righteousness reappears when he reminds his friends that he has never asked them for help for anything. His self-sufficient life-style is even more proof of his goodness. Convinced of his exemplary life, he challenges his friends to furnish evidence of his sins. Notice how he completes his statement by contrasting his "honest words" with his friends' arguments that go nowhere. Compared to his friends, Job is obviously superior.

> *Job 6:22-24 "Have I said, 'Give me something,' or, 'Offer a bribe for me from your wealth,' or, 'Deliver me from the hand of the adversary,' or, 'Redeem me from the hand of the tyrants'? Teach me, and I will be silent; and show me how I have erred.* NASU

Job believes his own message has been honest, but the words of Eliphaz have not come close to truth; his words are nothing but hot air from a despairing man. Throughout the heated conversation, Job maintains his innocence, and he insists that his friends are doing absolutely nothing to strengthen their relationship with him.

> *Job 6:25-27 "How forceful are honest words! But what does reproof from you reprove? Do you think that you can reprove words, when the speech of a despairing man is*

*wind? You would even cast lots over the fatherless, and bargain over your friend." * RSV

Studies in non-verbal communication have proven that the eyes are significant indicators of the sincerity and truthfulness of the one speaking. The pupils of the eye tend to constrict when one is telling a lie; on the other hand, the pupils generally dilate when truth is spoken. When one is reluctant to look another eye-to-eye, it is generally believed that the speaker is skirting the truth. Although listeners may not have taken courses in how to read the eyes when listening for the truth, somehow all have a built-in mechanism to look at the eyes to examine whether someone is being honest. Job appeals to his friends to study his eyes when he makes his claims of innocence. His reputation is at stake, and he wants his friends to believe in him.

*Job 6:28-30 "Look me in the eyes! Do you think I'd lie to your face? Think it over — no double-talk! Think carefully — my integrity is on the line! Can you detect anything false in what I say? Don't you trust me to discern good from evil?" * TM

JOB'S THIRD SPEECH

When Bildad informs Job concerning his belief that Job's suffering is taking place because of God's retribution for some hidden sin, Job stands firm that he is innocent:

*Job 9:20-21 "Though I am righteous, my mouth will condemn me; Though I am guiltless, he will declare me guilty. I am guiltless; I do not take notice of myself; I despise my life." * NAS

JOB'S FOURTH SPEECH

When Zophar declares Job's problems have occurred because of his wickedness, Job returns the barbs with criticisms of his opponents. What a piece of sarcasm Job lays on his friends! He belittles them as he opens his response to Zophar, stating that when they depart from life, all wisdom will disappear with them. In the following verses, Job refers to himself as being

84

righteous and blameless. The Narrator has claimed this, and God has confirmed this, but praise should come from others, not from self.

> *Job 12:2-5 Then Job replied: "Doubtless you are the people, and wisdom will die with you! But I have a mind as well as you; I am not inferior to you. Who does not know all these things? I have become a laughingstock to my friends, though I called upon God and he answered — a mere laughingstock, though righteous and blameless! Men at ease have contempt for misfortune as the fate of those whose feet are slipping."* NIV

Job is growing weary in listening to his three friends, and he is disgusted that his words are being ignored. He chastises his friends for acting as if they know more and are better than he. In this next statement he expresses these feelings and voices his desire to take his case to God. For Job to see himself as capable of confronting God says much about his arrogant nature.

> *Job 13:1-3 "Look, I have seen all this with my own eyes and heard it with my own ears, and now I understand. I know as much as you do. You are no better than I am. As for me, I would speak directly to the Almighty. I want to argue my case with God himself."* NLT

Zophar's speech had been full of platitudes, so Job counters by reeling off some of his own. Job makes a dynamic statement when he accuses his friends of whitewashing the truth with lies, and he labels them as "worthless physicians." An even stronger statement, dripping with sarcasm, is delivered when Job tells his friends their wisdom could be more readily seen if they just silenced themselves. This reminds me of the maxim, "It's better to remain silent and be thought of as a fool than to speak and remove all doubt." Someone has said, "Never overlook the opportunity to shut up." Job's friends were not convincing him they knew the secrets of life, so he pleads with them to hear his side of things.

> *Job 13:4-6 "As for you, you whitewash with lies; worthless physicians are you all. Oh that you would keep silent, and it would be your wisdom! Hear now my reasoning, and listen to the pleadings of my lips."* RSV

Job argues that his critics are not being fair in their judgment because they have taken sides without knowing the full truth. He claims that by arguing God's side with falsehoods, they are also showing partiality. Job has judged his share of cases, so he knows something about the evils of showing partiality. Job asks his friends how they would fare if God were to examine them. According to Job, his friends should fear God's judgment of them for their unfair treatment. He condemns the maxims offered by Zophar, calling them "proverbs of ashes," and labels the friends' arguments as "defenses of clay." According to Job, his friends do not have a clue:

> *Job 13:7-12   "Will you speak falsely for God, and speak deceitfully for him? Will you show partiality toward him, will you plead the case for God? Will it be well with you when he searches you out? Or can you deceive him, as one deceives a man? He will surely rebuke you if in secret you show partiality. Will not his majesty terrify you, and the dread of him fall upon you? Your maxims are proverbs of ashes, your defenses are defenses of clay."*   RSV

Job is using his friends as sounding boards as he prepares his case to present to God. His case will not be completed until he lays it out in *Job 31*; he assumes there are risks to take in presenting his case to God, but he is anxious for the moment because as he says below, "I am not godless" and "I will be proved innocent."   The Narrator has already told us Job was blameless and upright; now Job is taking up the case for himself.

> *Job 13:13-19   "Be silent now and leave me alone. Let me speak, and I will face the consequences. Yes, I will take my life in my hands and say what I really think. God might kill me, but I have no other hope. I am going to argue my case with him. But this is what will save me—I am not godless. If I were, I could not stand before him. Listen closely to what I am about to say. Hear me out. I have prepared my case; I will be proved innocent. Who can argue with me over this? And if you prove me wrong, I will remain silent and die."*
> NLT

JOB'S FIFTH SPEECH

After Eliphaz completes his second attempt to correct him, Job resumes his defense by ridiculing his friends' lengthy, repetitious comments, insisting that they have personal flaws he could attack. However, rather than dragging them through the mud, he assures them that he would take the high road and encourage them.

> *Job 16:1-5 Then Job answered: "I have heard many things like these. You are all painful comforters. Will your long-winded speeches never end? What makes you keep on arguing? I could also speak as you do if you were in my place. I could make great charges against you and shake my head at you. But instead, I would encourage you, and my words would bring you relief."* NCV

In other words, "Walk in my moccasins a mile, and then let's talk. In the dialogue below, Job ridicules the non-verbal behavior of his friends before turning the tables and labeling them as ungodly and wicked.

> *Job 16:10-11 "They gape at me with their mouth, they strike me reproachfully on the cheek, they gather together against me. God has delivered me to the ungodly, and turned me over to the hands of the wicked."* NKJV

After spending much time complaining about what God has done to him, he spends more time in preparing his case. His speech sometimes rambles as he drifts from talking about God to addressing God directly. In the middle of these mixed phrases, he continues to attack his three friends.

> *Job 17:10-12 "But, all of you, come and try again! I do not find a wise person among you. My days are gone, and my plans have been destroyed, along with the desires of my heart. These men think night is day; when it is dark, they say, 'Light is near.'"* NCV

If Job's friends are so ignorant they do not know the difference between night and day, how can they possibly know what is going on with him? This is another way Job rejects his friends' comments that "All will be better in the morning." Job's experience has thrown him into absolute darkness, and he sees no light at the end of the tunnel.

Job grows weary as his friends relentlessly attack. He gives a little ground in the sequence below by saying that any sin he has committed is none of their business. This is definitely a retreat of sorts because he has been demanding absolute purity. He demands that his friends can do him no more harm than God has already done.

> *Job 19:1 Then Job answered: "How long will you torment me, and beat me in pieces with words? These ten times you have cast reproach upon me; are you not ashamed to wrong me? And even if it is true that I have erred, my error remains with me. If indeed you magnify yourselves against me, and make my humiliation an argument against me, then know that God has put me in the wrong, and closed his net around me."* NRS

In previous speeches, Job has proclaimed his own righteousness. If good things are supposed to happen to good people and bad things to bad people, Job has gotten a raw deal. In all of Job's speeches, he never calls for mercy; after all, since he believes he is innocent, he wants justice. In his following comments, Job concludes that God has wronged him and has denied him deserved justice. God will later chastise Job for painting himself in the right and God in the wrong, but for now, observe Job's arrogance:

> *Job 19:4-7 "If it is true that I have gone astray, my error remains my concern alone. If indeed you would exalt yourselves above me and use my humiliation against me, then know that God has wronged me and drawn his net around me. Though I cry, 'I've been wronged!' I get no response; though I call for help, there is no justice."* NIV

In Job's mind, not only has God wronged him, but his friends have taken sides with God to humiliate him through their constant reproach. Job returns to his point in this next sequence of verses, as he calls for understanding and pity from his friends.

> *Job 19:19-21 "All my intimate friends abhor me, and those I have loved turn against me. My bones cling to my flesh, and I have escaped by the skin of my teeth. Have pity on me,*

have pity on me, O my friends, for the hand of God has touched me" NRS

Have you ever wondered where the phrase, "Skin of my teeth" originated? Well, here it is; Job's losses were so devastating that he had "escaped by the skin of his teeth." Job is convinced they are torturing an innocent man and will pay the price for their behavior. Job sends them the warning, "Judge not, lest you be judged."

Job 19:28-29 "If you say, 'How shall we persecute him?' And 'What pretext for a case against him can we find?' "Then be afraid of the sword for yourselves, for wrath brings the punishment of the sword, so that you may know there is judgment." NASU

JOB'S SEVENTH SPEECH

When Zophar completes his second speech, Job stands firm that his suffering is not due to God's retribution for sin. He once again insists that his complaint is against God, so they should just shut their mouths and listen to his comments directed at God.

Job 21:1-5 Then Job replied: "Listen carefully to my words; let this be the consolation you give me. Bear with me while I speak, and after I have spoken, mock on. Is my complaint directed to a human being? Why should I not be impatient? Look at me and be appalled; clap your hand over your mouth." TNIV

After blaming God for not punishing the wicked who deserve it, Job shames his friends for their comments that demean and belittle him.

Job 21:27-28 "Behold, I know your thoughts, and the plans by which you would wrong me. For you say, 'Where is the house of the nobleman, and where is the tent, the dwelling places of the wicked?'" NASU

Job next spends time explaining his observations of life, and he speaks of the knowledge of others whose understanding supports the truth of his conclusions. Job's observations and perceptions do not match those of the three friends when it comes to whether he fits the category of the wicked. Therefore, he rejects their thoughts as pure nonsense and absolute lies.

> *Job 21:29-34 "Have you not asked wayfaring men, And do you not recognize their witness? For the wicked is reserved for the day of calamity; they will be led forth at the day of fury. Who will confront him with his actions, and who will repay him for what he has done? While he is carried to the grave, men will keep watch over his tomb. The clods of the valley will gently cover him; moreover, all men will follow after him, while countless ones go before him. How then will you vainly comfort me, for your answers remain full of falsehood?"* NAS

JOB'S EIGHTH SPEECH

After Eliphaz makes his final attempt to prove God's retribution is at work, Job expresses his unhappiness that God refuses to appear to answer his questions and hear his case. He complains that he doesn't know where to find God and cannot go to His dwelling; in Job's mind this is more evidence of injustice. Job wants his one-on-one encounter with God and is convinced that once this happens God will see the error of His way.

> *Job 23:6-7 "Would he oppose me with great power? No, he would not press charges against me. There an upright man could present his case before him, and I would be delivered forever from my judge."* NIV

Job goes on to explain that he has searched for God in every conceivable direction, but God refuses to make His location known. On the other hand, God knows where Job is at all times; consequently, Job does not have equal status with God, an absolute injustice. Since God knows all things, surely when He realizes what He has done to an innocent man, He will rectify the situation.

> *Job 23:10-12 "But He knows the way I take; when He has tried me, I shall come forth as gold. My foot has held fast to His path; I have kept His way and not turned aside. I have not departed from the command of His lips; I have*

treasured the words of His mouth more than my necessary food." NASU

Job is displeased about God's ability to do whatever He pleases, with no one able to oppose His actions. It is clear that Job resents being treated as a finite creature by this infinite God!

> *Job 23:13 "But he stands alone, and who can oppose him? What his soul desires, even that he does."* WEB

Job's arrogance has been evidenced through his claims about himself, his contrast of self to the wicked, and his cries of injustice on the part of God. He ends his speech in response to Eliphaz by pointing out sins of others who go unpunished. As Job seeks equal status with God and demands God's answers to his questions and challenges, his case has been developing.

JOB'S NINTH AND FINAL SPEECH

Job opens his last round of comments in *Job 26* as he answers the accusations and challenges issued after Bildad's third speech. He returns to self-praise, asserting that nothing will shake his soul to the point of causing him to sin. He boasts that his integrity will remain intact and that his righteousness will not be tarnished:

> *Job 27:1-6 "As God lives, who has taken away my right, and the Almighty, who has made my soul bitter, as long as my breath is in me and the spirit of God is in my nostrils, my lips will not speak falsehood, and my tongue will not utter deceit. Far be it from me to say that you are right; until I die I will not put away my integrity from me. I hold fast my righteousness, and will not let it go; my heart does not reproach me for any of my days."* NRS

After detailing his complaint against God, Job draws the line between his upright nature and the wicked nature of his friends, driving the final nail and bending it that he will not admit to wrong-doing. On the other hand, he seems to put a curse on Eliphaz, Bildad, and Zophar for pitting themselves against him.

91

Job 27:7 "Let my enemy be as the wicked, and let him who rises up against me be as the unrighteous." ESV

Job spends most of his rebuttal after Eliphaz's speech dealing with concerns of God. He believes his knowledge of God's actions is far superior to that of his friends, so he takes it on himself to instruct and inform the three. However, before beginning his lesson on God, Job takes another swat at the arguments thrown his way:

> *Job 27:11-12 "But I am showing you the way that God works, making no secret of Shaddai's designs. And if you had all understood them for yourselves, you would not have wasted your breath in empty words."* NJB

Job expresses his longing for the days of old when he was revered by his peers. In Job's mind all of this was the way it was supposed to be, a righteous man enjoying the blessings he had earned and deserved.

> *Job 29:2-6 "Oh, that I were as in months past, as in the days when God watched over me; when His lamp shone upon my head, and when by His light I walked through darkness; just as I was in the days of my prime, when the friendly counsel of God was over my tent; when the Almighty was yet with me, when my children were around me; when my steps were bathed with cream, and the rock poured out rivers of oil for me!"* NKJV

The following dialogue is important because it reveals that Job must have been a judge to whom people turned for relief. Job remembers that his decisions have been respected because those in need received justice. This praise does not come from those who appeared before the city gates; rather, they come from the lips of Job as he admires himself.

> *Job 29:7-11 "Those were the days when I went to the city gate and took my place among the honored leaders. The young stepped aside when they saw me, and even the aged rose in respect at my coming. The princes stood in silence and put their hands over their mouths. The highest officials of the city stood quietly, holding their tongues in respect. All who heard me praised me. All who saw me spoke well of me."* NLT

In the following statement, notice the glowing terms Job uses to describe his righteous ways of judging those who came before his judgment seat. He claims his fair judgment caused others to give him great respect:

Job 29:12-17   "Because I delivered the poor who cried, and the orphan who had no helper. The blessing of the wretched came upon me, and I caused the widow's heart to sing for joy. I put on righteousness, and it clothed me; my justice was like a robe and a turban. I was eyes to the blind, and feet to the lame. I was a father to the needy, and I championed the cause of the stranger. I broke the fangs of the unrighteous, and made them drop their prey from their teeth."   NRS

When Job was enjoying health and wealth in the good old days, he was convinced his righteousness and public status would continue into infinity.

Job 29:18-20   "And I used to say, 'I shall die in honor, after days as numerous as the sand. My roots can reach the water, the dews of night settle on my leaves. My glory will be forever new and the bow in my hand for ever strong.'" NJB

Job continues admiring his own wisdom and his ability to communicate with others; he sees himself as being so highly esteemed that others felt truly blessed just to be in his presence. In the face of all his tragedies, Job's memories of the past fuel his Anger over the losses he has encountered.

Job 29:21-25   "They waited anxiously to hear me, and listened in silence to what I had to say. When I had finished, no one contradicted, my words dropping on them, one by one. They waited for me as though for rain, open-mouthed as though for a late shower. If I smiled at them, it was too good to be true; they watched my face for the least sign of favor. As their chief, I told them which course to take, like a king living among his troops, and I led them wherever I chose." NJB

Suddenly, Job's attitude toward others leaks out; he becomes incensed over how some have been treating him, so he expresses feelings he has held toward the fathers of those youngsters who were taunting him.

Job 30:1-2   "But now they make sport of me, those who are younger than I, whose fathers I would have disdained to set with the dogs of my flock.   What could I gain from the strength of their hands? All their vigor is gone." NRS

Job surely could have used help taking care of the dogs watching over his flocks, but he had no need for these incompetent people.   Job believes their poverty has led them into a lifestyle that has broken their health, and he has disdain for them because of their circumstances.   He has done nothing to help lift them out of the pit; however, now that he has lost all, he is Angry over the way others view him in his plight.   In the following passages Job describes the predicament faced by the impoverished.   How sad when one considers the vast amount of wealth Job could have used to alleviate some of their suffering.   Now Job is suffering, and others are treating him with disdain.   It is a reminder that "what goes around, comes around."

Job 30:3-15   "Through want and hard hunger they gnaw the dry and desolate ground, they pick mallow and the leaves of bushes, and to warm themselves the roots of broom.   They are driven out from society; people shout after them as after a thief.   In the gullies of wadis they must live, in holes in the ground, and in the rocks.   Among the bushes they bray; under the nettles they huddle together.   A senseless, disreputable brood, they have been whipped out of the land.   And now they mock me in song; I am a byword to them.   They abhor me, they keep aloof from me; they do not hesitate to spit at the sight of me.   Because God has loosed my bowstring and humbled me, they have cast off restraint in my presence.   On my right hand the rabble rise up; they send me sprawling, and build roads for my ruin. They break up my path, they promote my calamity; no one restrains them.   As through a wide breach they come; amid the crash they roll on.   Terrors are turned upon me; my honor is pursued as by the wind, and my prosperity has passed away like a cloud." NRS

As Job continues describing his misery, he claims to have wept for the poor and to have grieved over their condition; however, what does Job say about helping them rise above their circumstances?   Keep in mind that Job has already said he would not put them with his sheep dogs because they had nothing to offer him. He has no response other than to grieve and weep for them.

> *Job 30:25 "Did I not weep for those whose day was hard?*
> *Was not my soul grieved for the poor?"* NRS

Job takes great pride in noting that his eyes never wandered into lust. He believes the wicked should be punished, but he does not see himself in that category. If God would only take a closer look, surely He will see Job's integrity and reverse Job's circumstances.

> *Job 31:1-6 "I have made a covenant with my eyes; how then could I gaze at a virgin? And what is the portion of God from above or the heritage of the Almighty from on high? Is it not calamity to the unjust and disaster to those who work iniquity? Does He not see my ways and number all my steps? If I have walked with falsehood, and my foot has hastened after deceit, let Him weigh me with accurate scales, and let God know my integrity."* NASU

Imagine Job's claiming that if God were to weigh him with accurate scales, he would be exonerated! Job is going to go even further than this as he presents his case to God in *Job 31*, verses that will be considered in more detail in chapter 8 of this volume. Job presents hypothetical scenarios of sin, and he tells God what to do if he has committed any those evils. In effect, Job is claiming innocence of all the following sins:

- Straying from the way
- Letting his eyes guide his heart
- Placing his hands where they should not be
- Being enticed by a woman or lurking at a neighbor's door
- Failing to take care of claims brought by his servants
- Abusing or neglecting the poor, orphans, and widows
- Seeking gold and gloating over wealth
- Worshipping the sun and moon
- Rejoicing over the demise of an enemy
- Failing to take care of those around, both workers and aliens
- Trying to hide personal sins
- Neglecting to take care of those who work the land

Throughout Job's speeches, several stages of grief can be observed, but many of his feelings run together. This chapter has explored the Anger Job had concerning the efforts of his friends to attribute his suffering to hidden sins. Eliphaz, Bildad, and Zophar have no idea why Job lost his wealth and health, but their common belief is that disaster comes to the wicked. Therefore, their attempts to help Job by telling him to come clean are understandable, although wrong. Job's Anger is also easy to understand because he has seen too many wicked men who were faring well in life. This, simply put, does not seem fair to Job! While Anger appears to be a major motivator for the speeches Job aims at his friends, keep in mind that Job is also experiencing Depression, as does anyone wading through his or her own version of an "alligator pond."

STUDY GUIDE – Chapter 7

1. Discuss the struggle between the two spirits living within humans.

2. Has Job's blameless life led to an attitude problem?

3. Explain why Job rejects his friends' insistence that his sin has caused his suffering.

4. Why does Job urge his friends to look him in the eye?

5. What does Job believe he can offer God to improve His judgment?

6. Why is it a mistake for Job to seek justice rather than mercy?

7. Discuss Job's efforts to be on the same level with God.

8. How does Job view others who are suffering?

CHAPTER 8

– GOD IS GREAT, BUT HE HAS WRONGED ME!

Job's concepts and displeasure about God's works

Job's emotional roller-coaster becomes rather evident throughout his nine speeches, as he explains God's motives and actions, and then philosophizes over the marvels of the Almighty. At times he praises God, but then he stuns his friends with blatant criticism of his Creator. This chapter will explore the conversations of a man who puts his feelings and emotions on the table for all to examine.

Job's initial comments concerning God come seven days after he was plagued with sores covering his entire body. This complaint, found in *Job 3:3-26*, was covered and explored in chapter 4 of this volume. Eliphaz speaks after Job's tirade over his day of birth and his being left alive. In his second speech, Job identifies God as the source of his miseries.

> *Job 6:4 "The arrows of the Almighty are in me, my spirit drinks in their poison; God's terrors are marshaled against me."* NIV

Job is accurate in perceiving that God is in control of the catastrophes plaguing his life. The Narrator, in the first two chapters of the book of *Job*, tells of God's sending Satan with specific instructions to make Job's life miserable. In the last chapter of *Job*, the Narrator leaves no doubt about the source of disasters when he relates in *Job 42:11* that Job's brothers, sisters, and acquaintances "comforted and consoled him over all the trouble the Lord had brought upon him." The significance of that little statement has escaped many students of the Bible.

When one considers the number of verses in which Job refutes and condemns his friends, the verses in which he praises and defends himself, and the verses in which he speaks concerning God, the examination reveals that about 60% of the verses deal with his perception of God and his comments to God.

After Bildad claims Job's suffering is the result of God's retribution, Job responds with his understanding of God's power. The following eight verses contain recognition of God's greatness and powers, along with his recognition that God is beyond understanding. However, Job also voices frustration that he is not on the same level with God. Job would love to carry his complaint to the throne room, but he has no idea where to find God for such an encounter.

> *Job 9:3-11   "If one wished to dispute with Him, he could not answer Him once in a thousand times. Wise in heart and mighty in strength, who has defied Him without harm? It is God who removes the mountains, they know not how, when He overturns them in His anger; Who shakes the earth out of its place, and its pillars tremble; Who commands the sun not to shine, and sets a seal upon the stars; Who alone stretches out the heavens and tramples down the waves of the sea; Who makes the Bear, Orion and the Pleiades, and the chambers of the south; Who does great things, unfathomable, and wondrous works without number. Were He to pass by me, I would not see Him; were He to move past me, I would not perceive Him."* NASU

Job continues expressing his displeasure with God's superior position and His unwillingness to listen to a suffering saint. The hypothetical suffering person is an allusion to himself. Although Job believes he is innocent, he is convinced God has removed Himself from any consideration.

> *Job 9:12-16   "Were He to snatch away, who could restrain Him? Who could say to Him, 'What are You doing?' God will not turn back His anger; beneath Him crouch the helpers of Rahab. How then can I answer Him, and choose my words before Him? For though I were right, I could not answer; I would have to implore the mercy of my judge. If I called and He answered me, I could not believe that He was listening -to my voice."* NASU

Job continues with his complaint by claiming God has no reason to treat him in such a harsh way. He admits God is bigger and more powerful, but he is distressed that God uses this power on a guiltless man. If Job did not sin in what he said about God immediately following his losses, what is Job doing now when he says God "mocks the despair of the innocent"? Job also indicts God for destroying the righteous along with the wicked, and he flashes Anger that God has declared him guilty without a proper trial.

> *Job 9:17-24   "For He bruises me with a tempest and multiplies my wounds without cause. He will not allow me to get my breath, but saturates me with bitterness. If it is a matter of power, behold, He is the strong one! And if it is a matter of justice, who can summon Him?   Though I am righteous, my mouth will condemn me; though I am guiltless, He will declare me guilty. I am guiltless; I do not take notice of myself; I despise my life. It is all one; therefore I say, 'He destroys the guiltless and the wicked.'   If the scourge kills suddenly, He mocks the despair of the innocent. The earth is given into the hand of the wicked; He covers the faces of its judges. If it is not He, then who is it?"* NASU

Job often drifts from talking about God to making comments to God. After brief comments to God, Job pauses to collect his thoughts as he considers issues aimed at Bargaining, a normal stage of the grieving process. Three thoughts are considered: 1) He knows God is not human, and this limits his insights into how to present his case. 2) He considers the need for a mediator to plead his cause. 3) Job desires that God release His grip and allow him to come before the heavenly throne for a personal hearing.

> *Job 9:32-35 "God is not a mortal like me, so I cannot argue with him or take him to trial. If only there were a mediator between us, someone who could bring us together. The mediator could make God stop beating me, and I would no longer live in terror of his punishment. Then I could speak to him without fear, but I cannot do that in my own strength."* NLT

Zophar becomes irate after listening to Job's claims, so he steps in to attack Job for refusing to come clean with whatever has brought on God's retribution. Job sees wicked people around him who carry carved gods, yet they are doing fine. This he sees as evidence of God's injustice, so Job indicts God once again because these evil people live in better circumstances than he is experiencing.

> *Job 12:6 "The tents of robbers are at peace, and those who provoke God are secure, who bring their god in their hands."* NRS

Zophar has praised God, but he also has claimed that Job is unable to fathom the mysteries of God. This is turning into a bloody contest, and Job isn't about to leave that comment standing without comment. Job claims his knowledge about God can certainly compete with that of his three friends. There is no dispute over who is responsible for Job's suffering; the dispute is over why the suffering is taking place.

> *Job 12:7-12 "But now ask the beasts, and let them teach you; and the birds of the heavens, and let them tell you. Or speak to the earth, and let it teach you; and let the fish of the sea declare to you. Who among all these does not know that the hand of the Lord has done this, in whose hand is the life of every living thing, and the breath of all mankind? Does not the ear test words, as the palate tastes its food? Wisdom is with aged men, with long life is understanding."* NASU

Job continues countering his friends' explanations of the Almighty with his understanding of God's powers that are sometimes destructive. Man has no way to overcome or counter the strength and wisdom of God. While Job recognizes God's power, there is still an underlying displeasure with man's inability to confront and respond to the Almighty.

> *Job 12:13-16 "With Him are wisdom and strength, He has counsel and understanding. If He breaks a thing down, it cannot be rebuilt; if He imprisons a man, there can be no release. If He withholds the waters, they dry up; if He sends them out, they overwhelm the earth. With Him are strength and prudence. The deceived and the deceiver are His."* NKJV

After Job counters Zophar by claiming he knows as much as his three friends, his complaint against God is renewed. In the good old days, Job was once a mighty prince, but he has been plundered and has become a laughingstock among those who once respected him. When he speaks about "princes, trusted ones, elders, mighty, and chiefs" in the following verses, he alludes to himself as the suffering party. He presents this as further evidence that God is unfair. He has been struck by the hand of God and is groping for the way out of the "alligator pond."

> *Job 12:17-25 "He leads counselors away plundered, and makes fools of the judges. He loosens the bonds of kings, and binds their waist with a belt. He leads princes away plundered, and overthrows the mighty. He deprives the trusted ones of speech, and takes away the discernment of the elders. He pours contempt on princes, and disarms the mighty. He uncovers deep things out of darkness, and brings the shadow of death to light. He makes nations great, and destroys them; He enlarges nations, and guides them. He takes away the understanding of the chiefs of the people of the earth, and makes them wander in a pathless wilderness. They grope in the dark without light, and He makes them stagger like a drunken man."* NKJV

Job becomes distraught while trying to reason with his friends, so he repeats his desire for an opportunity to present his arguments to God.

> *Job 13:3 But I would speak to the Almighty, and I desire to argue my case with God.* RSV

Job expresses no fear in coming before the Lord with his complaint; on the other hand, a godless man would not dare be so bold.

> *Job 13:15-16 "Behold, he will slay me; I have no hope; yet I will defend my ways to his face. This will be my salvation, that a godless man shall not come before him."* RSV

Nobody manages to move Job through the first round of debate, so Eliphaz returns in another attempt to set Job straight. When Eliphaz finishes his dialogue, Job issues even further complaints and criticisms toward God. Job refers to God as his opponent, and he accuses God of throwing a righteous man into the hands of Satan.

> *Job 16:6-11 "God assails me and tears me in his anger and gnashes his teeth at me; my opponent fastens on me his*

piercing eyes. People open their mouths to jeer at me; they strike my cheek in scorn and unite together against me. God has turned me over to the ungodly and thrown me into the clutches of the wicked." TNIV

According to Job, he was doing fine until God stepped into his path and showed him no pity. Ironically, Job refers to pity and mercy at times, but he never asks for God's mercy. Job demands justice because he is convinced he is right and God is wrong.

> *Job 16:12-14 "All was well with me, but he shattered me; he seized me by the neck and crushed me. He has made me his target; his archers surround me. Without pity, he pierces my kidneys and spills my gall on the ground. Again and again he bursts upon me; he rushes at me like a warrior."* TNIV

After Bildad's second scolding, Job makes it very clear that God is wrong and justice is blind. He accuses God of removing him from his treasured social status, destroying his hope, making him an enemy, and driving a wedge between him and his friends. It's all God's fault!

> *Job 19:6-13 "Know then that God has wronged me, and has closed His net around me. Behold, I cry, 'Violence!' but I get no answer; I shout for help, but there is no justice. He has walled up my way so that I cannot pass; and He has put darkness on my paths. He has stripped my honor from me, and removed the crown from my head. He breaks me down on every side, and I am gone; and He has uprooted my hope like a tree. He has also kindled His anger against me, and considered me as His enemy. His troops come together, and build up their way against me, and camp around my tent. He has removed my brothers far from me and my acquaintances are completely estranged from me."* NAS

> *Job 19:21 "Pity me, pity me, O you my friends, for the hand of God has struck me."* NAS

Job has now called God his opponent, and he has identified himself as God's enemy. He has said God wronged him and has not dispensed proper justice. After Zophar presents his second attempt to correct him, Job gives more evidence of God's injustice—wicked people around him are doing fine.

> *Job 21:6-15 "When I think of it I am dismayed, and shuddering seizes my flesh. Why do the wicked live on, reach old age, and grow mighty in power? Their children are established in their presence, and their offspring before their eyes. Their houses are safe from fear, and no rod of God is upon them. Their bull breeds without fail; their cow calves and never miscarries. They send out their little ones like a flock, and their children dance around. They sing to the tambourine and the lyre, and rejoice to the sound of the pipe. They spend their days in prosperity, and in peace they go down to Sheol. They say to God, 'Leave us alone! We do not desire to know your ways. What is the Almighty that we should serve him? And what profit do we get if we pray to him?'"* NRS

Job questions why these people go unpunished. Perhaps he has heard the maxim that the fathers eat the grapes and set their children's teeth on edge. Job's phrase for it is "God stores up their iniquity for their children."

> *Job 21:16-19 "Is not their prosperity indeed their own achievement? The plans of the wicked are repugnant to me. How often is the lamp of the wicked put out? How often does calamity come upon them? How often does God distribute pains in his anger? How often are they like straw before the wind, and like chaff that the storm carries away? You say, 'God stores up their iniquity for their children.'"* NRS

Job is not satisfied in hearing that children will suffer for their parents' sins; he wants the guilty parties to suffer. If Job could only instruct God concerning judgment principles, things would surely improve.

> *Job 21:20-26 "Let it be paid back to them, so that they may know it. Let their own eyes see their destruction, and let them drink of the wrath of the Almighty. For what do they care for their household after them, when the number of their months is cut off? Will any teach God knowledge,*

seeing that he judges those that are on high? One dies in full prosperity, being wholly at ease and secure, his loins full of milk and the marrow of his bones moist. Another dies in bitterness of soul, never having tasted of good. They lie down alike in the dust, and the worms cover them." NRS

When Eliphaz speaks for the third time, Job renews his complaint that God has not appeared to hear his case. He is convinced that God would find him guiltless if He heard the facts, but Job doesn't know how to find the Almighty to impart the information.

Job 23:2-9 "Even today my complaint is bitter; his hand is heavy in spite of my groaning. If only I knew where to find him; if only I could go to his dwelling! I would state my case before him and fill my mouth with arguments. I would find out what he would answer me, and consider what he would say. Would he oppose me with great power? No, he would not press charges against me. There an upright man could present his case before him, and I would be delivered forever from my judge. But if I go to the east, he is not there; if I go to the west, I do not find him. When he is at work in the north, I do not see him; when he turns to the south, I catch no glimpse of him." NIV

Job wants a level playing field on which to face God with evidence of his faithfulness. Job decries the fact that he does not know where to find God, while God knows his every step, placing Job at a huge disadvantage. According to Job, God does whatever He pleases, disregarding the upright nature of the one under attack -- namely himself.

Job 23:10-17 "But he knows the way that I take; when he has tested me, I will come forth as gold. My feet have closely followed his steps; I have kept to his way without turning aside. I have not departed from the commands of his lips; I have treasured the words of his mouth more than my daily bread. But he stands alone, and who can oppose him? He does whatever he pleases. He carries out his decree against me, and many such plans he still has in store. That is why I am terrified before him; when I think of all this, I fear him. God has made my heart faint; the Almighty has terrified me. Yet I am not silenced by the darkness, by the thick darkness that covers my face." NIV

Job's desire for equality with God appears once more when he laments God's knowledge of judgment day, while people are not informed. He furthers his complaint about injustices he does not believe God addresses.

> *Job 24:1-4 "But if Judgment Day isn't hidden from the Almighty, why are we kept in the dark? There are people out there getting by with murder — stealing and lying and cheating. They rip off the poor and exploit the unfortunate, push the helpless into the ditch, bully the weak so that they fear for their lives."* TM

Job was once the richest man in the East; he had the resources to assist the poor in many ways. However, he dresses down God for seeing the condition of those in poverty and acting as if nothing is wrong. Job's heart aches for these poor, suffering people. Job's sympathy appears to be for others, but he deplores the failure of God to alleviate his own pain and agony.

> *Job 24:5-12 "The poor, like stray dogs and cats, scavenge for food in back alleys. They sort through the garbage of the rich, eke out survival on handouts. Homeless, they shiver through cold nights on the street; they've no place to lay their heads. Exposed to the weather, wet and frozen, they huddle in makeshift shelters. Nursing mothers have their babies snatched from them; the infants of the poor are kidnapped and sold. They go about patched and threadbare; even the hard workers go hungry. No matter how back-breaking their labor, they can never make ends meet. People are dying right and left, groaning in torment. The wretched cry out for help and God does nothing, acts like nothing's wrong!"* TM

Job continues his harangue against God's ways by furnishing more examples of injustice. These concern Gods' allowing ungodly kinds of acts to go unpunished, while coming down on a godly man such as himself.

> *Job 24:13-17 "Then there are those who avoid light at all costs, who scorn the light-filled path. When the sun goes*

*down, the murderer gets up — kills the poor and robs the
defenseless. Sexual predators can't wait for nightfall,
thinking, 'No one can see us now.' Burglars do their work
at night, but keep well out of sight through the day. They
want nothing to do with light. Deep darkness is morning for
that bunch; they make the terrors of darkness their
companions in crime."* TM

Job proceeds to give his description of these poor, suffering people,
using very unsavory terms to describe them. If he has seen suffering people
in this light, are we puzzled that others are now viewing him in the same
light with which he has judged? Job has determined that these wretched
people are getting exactly what they deserved.

*Job 24:18-21 "Yet they are foam on the surface of the
water; their portion of the land is cursed, so that no one goes
to the vineyards. As heat and drought snatch away the
melted snow, so the grave snatches away those who have
sinned. The womb forgets them, the worm feasts on them;
the wicked are no longer remembered but are broken like a
tree. They prey on the barren and childless woman, and to
the widow show no kindness."* TNIV

Does the passage above remind the reader of the words of Jesus about
making judgmental statements about others?

*Matthew 7:1-2 "Do not judge so that you will not be judged.
For in the way you judge, you will be judged; and by your
standard of measure, it will be measured to you."* NASU

Job vacillates all over the place about God's failure to punish evil and
God's punishment of evil. In the passage below, he agrees that God has done
well in punishing the wicked, but he sees himself as undeserving of
suffering. His once secure life and wealth should have been viewed as
evidence that he was upright; the passage below presents Job's further claim
of God's injustice.

*Job 24:22-25 "But he who lays mighty hold on tyrants rises
up to take away a life that seemed secure. He let him build
his hopes on false security, but kept his eyes on every step he
took. He had his time of glory, now he vanishes, wilting like*

the saltwort once it is picked, and withering like an ear of corn. Is this not so? Who can prove me a liar or show that my words have no substance?" NJB

After the last of the friends' speeches is delivered by Bildad, Job once again informs his friends about the work of God. He is not about to take a back seat when it comes to a display of knowledge about God. He opens his ninth dialogue by saying that God is the only One who understands Sheol (the grave) and Abaddon (the destroyer):

Job 26:5-14 "The departed spirits tremble under the waters and their inhabitants. Naked is Sheol before Him and Abaddon has no covering. He stretches out the north over empty space, and hangs the earth on nothing. He wraps up the waters in His clouds; and the cloud does not burst under them. He obscures the face of the full moon, and spreads His cloud over it. He has inscribed a circle on the surface of the waters, at the boundary of light and darkness. The pillars of heaven tremble, and are amazed at His rebuke. He quieted the sea with His power, and by His understanding He shattered Rahab. By His breath the heavens are cleared; His hand has pierced the fleeing serpent. Behold, these are the fringes of His ways; and how faint a word we hear of Him! But His mighty thunder, who can understand?" NASU

Job has questions concerning God's retribution, and he puzzles over whether God responds to the cry of the godless or whether the godless even call upon God.

Job 27:7-9 "For what is the hope of the godless when God cuts them off, when God takes away their lives? Will God hear their cry when trouble comes upon them? Will they take delight in the Almighty? Will they call upon God at all times?" NRS

The following passage has puzzled many Bible scholars; some believe this passage is the missing third speech of Zophar. In fact, the New Jerusalem Bible presents it this way because the speech seems to further the case of the three friends who have claimed that tragedies are a result of

God's retribution. Rather than being the third speech of Zophar, perhaps Job is simply claiming this is the way things ought to be—the wicked are the ones who should be punished. Job does not see himself as fitting that category. Many other comments by Job substantiate the thought that Job doesn't believe God is dispensing true justice. Understood in this way, Job is expressing his disapproval of God's decision to treat him as the wicked should be treated.

> *Job 27:13-23* *"This is the fate that God assigns to the wicked, the inheritance that the violent receive from Shaddai. Though he have many children, it is but for the sword; his descendants will never have enough to eat. Plague will bury those he leaves behind him, and their widows will have no chance to mourn them. Though he amass silver like dust and gather fine clothes like clay, let him gather! Some good man will wear them, while his silver is shared among the upright. All he has built himself is a spider's web, made himself a watchman's shack. He goes to bed rich, but never again: he wakes to find it has all gone. Terror assails him in broad daylight, and at night a whirlwind sweeps him off. An east wind picks him up and drags him away, snatching him up from his homestead. Pitilessly he is turned into a target, and forced to flee from the hands that menace him. His downfall is greeted with applause; he is hissed wherever he goes."* NJB

Job must have believed it very important to display his knowledge of life to his friends, for he spends quite some time philosophizing about things that are hidden from view. God has placed some things within the earth for man to search and find, and they are within human reach and understanding. Minerals, jewels, and ore are imbedded in the earth, but humans have been able to discover and mine them because God has made provisions for this to take place.

> *Job 28:1-11* *"There are mines where people dig silver and places where gold is made pure. Iron is taken from the ground, and copper is melted out of rocks. Miners bring lights and search deep into the mines for ore in thick darkness. Miners dig a tunnel far from where people live,*

where no one has ever walked; they work far from people, swinging and swaying from ropes. Food grows on top of the earth, but below ground things are changed as if by fire. Sapphires are found in rocks, and gold dust is also found there. No hawk knows that path; the falcon has not seen it. Proud animals have not walked there, and no lions cross over it. Miners hit the rocks of flint and dig away at the bottom of the mountains. They cut tunnels through the rock and see all the treasures there. They search for places where rivers begin and bring things hidden out into the light." NCV

After evidencing his knowledge of hidden things God has permitted to come to light, he contrasts this with wisdom that God has hidden from mankind. Job acknowledges God's works, but in doing so, he also points out man's inability to understand the wisdom of God. Does this include Job? He should listen to himself, for he frequently counters this thought by making claims that question God's wisdom in dealing with his servant Job.

Job 28:12-22   "But where shall wisdom be found? And where is the place of understanding. Mortals do not know the way to it, and it is not found in the land of the living. The deep says, 'It is not in me,' and the sea says, 'It is not with me.' It cannot be gotten for gold, and silver cannot be weighed out as its price. It cannot be valued in the gold of Ophir, in precious onyx or sapphire. Gold and glass cannot equal it, nor can it be exchanged for jewels of fine gold. No mention shall be made of coral or of crystal; the price of wisdom is above pearls. The chrysolite of Ethiopia cannot compare with it, nor can it be valued in pure gold. Where then does wisdom come from? And where is the place of understanding? It is hidden from the eyes of all living, and concealed from the birds of the air. Abaddon and Death [the destroyer and his offspring death] say, 'We have heard a rumor of it with our ears.'" NRS

Job completes his philosophical point by saying wisdom belongs only to God. He is tiring of his friends' claim to superior knowledge; however, as mentioned earlier, he also erodes his own claims to knowledge.

Job 28:23-28 "God has knowledge of the way to it, and of its resting-place; for his eyes go to the ends of the earth, and he sees everything under heaven. When he made a weight for the wind, measuring out the waters; when he made a law for the rain, and a way for the thunder-flames; then he saw it, and put it on record; he gave it its fixed form, searching it out completely. And he said to man, 'Truly the fear of the Lord is wisdom, and to keep from evil is the way to knowledge.'" BBE

After heaping praises on himself and airing his disdain for people he deems lower than himself, Job once again complains about the way God has treated him.

Job 30:18-19 "In his great power God grabs hold of my clothing his great power and chokes me with the collar of my coat. He throws me into the mud, and I become like dirt and ashes." NCV

Job's view of the way life should work was just not taking place. Why was God not watching him more closely to see the righteous path he had taken?

Job 31:2-4 "For what is man's lot from God above, his heritage from the Almighty on high? Is it not ruin for the wicked, disaster for those who do wrong? Does he not see my ways and count my every step?" NIV

Job's comments about God reveal more of his arrogant attitude that God was addressing through tribulation. Now that we have contemplated the words of Job concerning God, both positive and negative thoughts, the next chapter will focus on Job's comments made to the Lord.

STUDY GUIDE – Chapter 8

1. Was Job correct in claiming God was behind his suffering?

2. How significant is Job's reference to constellations in Job 9:9?

3. On what does Job base his claim that God has wronged him?

4. Job recognizes God's wisdom; why does he condemn God's actions?

5. How does Job use his desire to come before God as evidence of his innocence?

6. What is Job's idea of justice found in Job 21:20-26?

7. Discuss Job's desire to confront God on equal footing.

8. How consistent is Job's claim that God does not punish the wicked?

CHAPTER 9

– THIS IS THE WAY THINGS OUGHT TO BE!

Job tells the Creator how to judge His creation.

Job was speaking to his friends after Eliphaz's first speech, but early in his comments, Job speaks directly to God. He laments over the fact that his life is effectively over; he even reminds God (as if God doesn't know what is happening) that he will soon be gone.

> *Job 7:7-10 "Remember, God, that my life is only a breath. My eyes will never see happy times again. Remember, God, that my life is only a breath. My eyes will never see happy times again. Those who see me now will see me no more; you will look for me, but I will be gone. As a cloud disappears and is gone, people go to the grave and never return. They will never come back to their houses again, and their places will not know them anymore."* NCV

Job continues his message to God by saying he will remain quiet no longer. He cannot even have a night's rest because of the disturbing visions he claims God sends in the middle of the night. He may have held his tongue for seven days after losing his health, but Job is now determined to voice his complaint and does so in the following passage:

> *Job 7:11-16 "And so I'm not keeping one bit of this quiet, I'm laying it all out on the table; my complaining to high heaven is bitter, but honest. Are you going to put a muzzle on me, the way you quiet the sea and still the storm? If I say, 'I'm going to bed, then I'll feel better. A little nap will lift my spirits,' you come and so scare me with nightmares and frighten me with ghosts that I'd rather strangle in the bed clothes than face this kind of life any longer. I hate this*

life! Who needs any more of this? Leave me alone! There's nothing to my life — it's nothing but smoke." TM

Job tries to communicate with God on a human level. He is convinced God has better things to do than pick on him. Job refers to his sin only in hypothetical terms; even if has sinned, he chides God for being so harsh. He demands that God leave him alone, and he chastises God for singling him out for the kind of treatment he is receiving. Statements made in Anger are definitely not pleas for mercy. Mercy is called for from the knees with open hands; demands are made from the feet with a closed fist. He warns that God will be sorry when He looks around and cannot find his suffering servant.

> *Job 7:17-21 "What are human beings, that you make so much of them, that you set your mind on them, visit them every morning, test them every moment? Will you not look away from me for a while; leave me alone until I swallow my spittle? If I sin, what do I do to you, you watcher of humanity? Why have you made me your target? Why have I become a burden to you? Why do you not pardon my transgression and take away my iniquity? For now I shall lie in the earth; you will seek me, but I shall not be."* NRS

After Bildad's first speech, Job has more to say to God, and his Depression and frustration are quite evident. All efforts to find relief have gained no ground, so Job concludes that all is futile because his life is in ruins.

> *Job 9:28-31 "I am afraid of all my sufferings; I know that You will not hold me innocent. If I am condemned, why then do I labor in vain? If I wash myself with snow water, and cleanse my hands with soap, yet You will plunge me into the pit, and my own clothes will abhor me."* NKJV

After expressing frustration over God's refusal to give him a hearing, Job heats up the message by questioning what charges God has to bring against him. He pleads this part of the case based on the inequities that exist in his effort for relief, so he ponders whether God has human eyes to understand. Job chides God for what is taking place, claiming God knows he is innocent. Job concludes that God is the one who made him and blessed him, so if he has imperfections, it must be the Creator's fault.

Job 10:2-12 "I say to God: 'Do not declare me guilty, but tell me what charges you have against me. Does it please you to oppress me, to spurn the work of your hands, while you smile on the plans of the wicked? Do you have eyes of flesh? Do you see as a mortal sees? Are your days like those of a mortal or your years like those of a human being that you must search out my faults and probe after my sin—though you know that I am not guilty and that no one can rescue me from your hand? Your hands shaped me and made me. Will you now turn and destroy me? Remember that you molded me like clay. Will you now turn me to dust again? Did you not pour me out like milk and curdle me like cheese, clothe me with skin and flesh and knit me together with bones and sinews? You gave me life and showed me kindness, and in your providence watched over my spirit.'" TNIV

Job further berates God for singling him out for harsh treatment that he considers absolutely undeserved.

Job 10:13-17 "But this is what you concealed in your heart, and I know that this was in your mind: If I sinned, you would be watching me and would not let my offense go unpunished. If I am guilty—woe to me! Even if I am innocent, I cannot lift my head, for I am full of shame and drowned in my affliction. If I hold my head high, you stalk me like a lion and again display your awesome power against me. You bring new witnesses against me and increase your anger toward me; your forces come against me wave upon wave." TNIV

Job ends this speech by returning to his opening expressions of Anger found in *Job 3*; asking God, "Why was I born in the first place?" He hopes his remaining days are few; Job is ready to die to end his gloom.

Job 10:18-22 "Why then did you bring me out of the womb? I wish I had died before any eye saw me. If only I had never come into being, or had been carried straight from the womb to the grave! Are not my few days almost over? Turn away from me so I can have a moment's joy before I go to the

117

place of no return, to the land of gloom and utter darkness to the land of deepest night, of utter darkness and disorder, where even the light is like darkness." TNIV

After Zophar's first speech, Job spends the early part of his response attacking his friends and showing his superior knowledge of God's works. However, he also has more to say to God with the following Bargaining statements.

Job 13:20-22 "Only two things do not do to me, then I will not hide from Your face: remove Your hand from me, and let not the dread of You terrify me. Then call, and I will answer; or let me speak, then reply to me." NASU

Job continues demanding that God reveal what he has against him, and he chides God for hiding from him. Notice in the passage below that he refers to God as his enemy. Earlier Job referred to God as his opponent, both statements are efforts to be on equal ground with God, but his labeling of the relationship is rather alarming! In his comments, Job really gives God a scolding.

Job 13:23-28 "How many are my iniquities and sins? Make known to me my rebellion and my sin. Why do You hide Your face and consider me Your enemy? Will You cause a driven leaf to tremble? Or will You pursue the dry chaff? For You write bitter things against me and make me to inherit the iniquities of my youth. You put my feet in the stocks and watch all my paths; You set a limit for the soles of my feet, while I am decaying like a rotten thing, like a garment that is moth-eaten." NASU

At times it appears Job is informing the Creator about man's frailties and weaknesses. He is disturbed because God determines all things with humans having no voice in the matter, another attempt to have equality with his Creator.

Job 14:1-6 "How frail is humanity! How short is life, how full of trouble! We blossom like a flower and then wither. Like a passing shadow, we quickly disappear. Must you keep an eye on such a frail creature and demand an accounting from me? Who can bring purity out of an

impure person? No one! You have decided the length of our lives. You know how many months we will live, and we are not given a minute longer. So leave us alone and let us rest! We are like hired hands, so let us finish our work in peace." NLT

Job's feelings of Depression deepen as he observes that trees live again after being cut down, while people die and exist no more on earth. In most of the sequence below, Job seems to believe mankind has no after-life; however, his doubts diminish a little when he refers to rising once the heavens are no more.

Job 14:7-12 "At least there is hope for a tree: if it is cut down, it will sprout again, and its new shoots will not fail. Its roots may grow old in the ground and its stump die in the soil, yet at the scent of water it will bud and put forth shoots like a plant. But man dies and is laid low; he breathes his last and is no more. As water disappears from the sea or a riverbed becomes parched and dry, so man lies down and does not rise; till the heavens are no more, men will not awake or be roused from their sleep." NIV

Notice how Job's complaint continues as he asks to be hidden in the grave until God's anger subsides. This sounds like he believes in a resurrection; however, he follows this by questioning whether man will rise again. Job believes an answer to this question would give him some measure of hope. He has made many statements concerning his purity, but he also wavers on this by seeming to admit his human imperfection.

Job 14:13-17 "I wish you would hide me in the grave and forget me there until your anger has passed. But mark your calendar to think of me again! Can the dead live again? If so, this would give me hope through all my years of struggle, and I would eagerly await the release of death. You would call and I would answer, and you would yearn for me, your handiwork. For then you would guard my steps, instead of watching for my sins. My sins would be sealed in a pouch, and you would cover my guilt." NLT

119

Any lack of hope, according to Job, is caused by God's actions. As people age, God disfigures them and sends them to their death. Because they depart from life, they don't even know what happens in their children's future. In Job's eyes, it is plain to see that God is simply unfair.

> *Job 14:18-22 "But the mountain falling comes to nothing; the rock is removed out of its place; the waters wear the stones; the torrents of it wash away the dust of the earth. So you destroy the hope of man. You forever prevail against him, and he passes; You change his face, and send him away. His sons come to honor, and he doesn't know it; they are brought low, but he doesn't perceive it of them. But his flesh on him has pain; his soul within him mourns."* WEB

As he listens to Eliphaz speak for the second time, Job grows sick and tired of his friends' accusations, so he calls on God to deal with them. Earlier he commended himself for not rejoicing if an enemy died, but he has no problem indicating God should inflict punishment on his friends.

> *Job 17:3-5 "Give me, O God, the pledge you demand. Who else will put up security for me? You have closed their minds to understanding; therefore, you will not let them triumph. If people denounce their friends for reward, the eyes of their children will fail."* TNIV

Job's last comments in his attempt to correct God are found after Bildad's third speech. He refers to his efforts to confront the Almighty, but claims God's acts have shown no mercy. It is ironic that Job never asks for mercy; he earlier claimed there was no mercy, and he says something similar here in that God has shown no mercy.

> *Job 30:20-23 "I cry out to you God, but you do not answer. I stand up, but you just look at me. You have turned on me without mercy, with your powerful hand you attacked me. You snatched me up and threw me into the wind and tossed me about in the storm. I know you will bring me down to death to the place where all living people must go."* NCV

In chapter 7 of this volume, we examined Job's list of sins he believed should be punished, along with the proper penalty. Our focus at that time was on his arrogance in claiming he was not guilty of any the transgressions.

Job 31:1-4 opens with Job's praising himself and criticizing God's failure to take note of his goodness. He then addresses God with a list of hypothetical sins and the proper punishment for each. In reading this list of sins, notice that two points are found within each. First, because Job says "If I have these things," he is suggesting his innocence; secondly, listing the proper punishments is a direct criticism of God's ability to know how to judge. As earlier indicated, Job had been a respected judge who settled disputes between fellow men. This human judge now presumes to inform the Creator and Judge of all humanity how to properly judge and how to distribute punishment.

The passage below is one of those in which Job seems to vary between talking about God and speaking directly to God. To stay with the context of the passage, all hypothetical sins within this chapter are treated as his comments to God. Job has made some efforts at Bargaining with God along the way when he refers to the need for a mediator and his desire for his sufferings to be written on a scroll for others to read. Much of what he says is a form of Bargaining because he lets God know the proper consequences for certain behavior. What an accusation against God to say the Almighty needs to weigh him on accurate scales to recognize his integrity!

> *Job 31:5-8 "If I have been dishonest or lied to others, then let God weigh me on honest scales. Then he will know I have done nothing wrong. If I have turned away from doing what is right, or my heart has been led by my eyes to do wrong, or my hands have been made unclean, then let other people eat what I have planted, and let my crops be plowed up."* NCV

Job knows of men who have been unfaithful to their wives; however, he has not been seduced into adultery, nor has he seduced his neighbor's wife.

> *Job 31:9-12 "If my heart has been seduced by a woman, or if I have lurked at my neighbor's door, let my wife go and grind for someone else, let others have intercourse with her! For I would have committed a sin of lust, a crime punishable by the law, a fire, indeed, burning all to Perdition, which would have devoured my whole revenue."* NJB

In the passage above, Job is beginning to put together a judgment manual of sins and the appropriate punishment for each. Each of us could put together a list of sins we have avoided, and in so doing, we could identify people who have sinned in that way more than yours truly. Job's manual of transgressions grows as he continues listing sins he has avoided. Job's wording is interesting; he says he listened to his servants' grievances against him, so it seems his servants have had issues with him. Job has aided the widows, orphans, and those in poverty; furthermore, he claims he has not denied justice to an orphan even though others around him may have encouraged his doing so. Can you hear Job chastising God throughout these verses? In effect he is saying to God, "I was fair in judgment when witnesses presented corrupted testimony in my hearing; why are You listening and favoring my friends by taking their side?" In the passage below, a summary of his basic message would be as follows: "Bring it on if I have not treated servants, widows, orphans, and the poor kindly by helping meet their needs."

> *Job 31:13-23 "If I have despised the claim of my male or female slaves when they filed a complaint against me, what then could I do when God arises, and when He calls me to account, what will I answer Him? Did not He who made me in the womb make him, and the same one fashion us in the womb? If I have kept the poor from their desire, or have caused the eyes of the widow to fail, or have eaten my morsel alone, and the orphan has not shared it (but from my youth he grew up with me as with a father, and from infancy I guided her), if I have seen anyone perish for lack of clothing, or that the needy had no covering, if his loins have not thanked me, and if he has not been warmed with the fleece of my sheep, if I have lifted up my hand against the orphan, because I saw I had support in the gate, let my shoulder fall from the socket, and my arm be broken off at the elbow. For calamity from God is a terror to me, and because of His majesty I can do nothing." NAS*

God had blessed Job with more material wealth than any of his peers, so Job claims he has not made money his god. He then takes pride in the fact that he has never worshiped the sun or moon. If Job had ever put other gods ahead of the Living God, he is ready to suffer the consequences.

122

Job 31:24-28 "If I have put my confidence in gold, and called fine gold my trust, if I have gloated because my wealth was great, and because my hand had secured so much; if I have looked at the sun when it shone, or the moon going in splendor, and my heart became secretly enticed, and my hand threw a kiss from my mouth, that too would have been an iniquity calling for judgment, for I would have denied God above." NAS

Job praises himself for never rejoicing when an enemy suffered; he has never asked for his enemy's life to be taken. Furthermore, Job has taken care of strangers who came his way.

Job 31:29-32 "Have I rejoiced at the extinction of my enemy, or exulted when evil befell him? No, I have not allowed my mouth to sin by asking for his life in a curse. Have the men of my tent not said, 'Who can find one who has not been satisfied with his meat'? The alien has not lodged outside, for I have opened my doors to the traveler." NAS

Job claims he has no secret sins and that his life has been open for anyone to examine; he was certainly not like Adam who tried to hide after sinning against God. Many people are driven to action of one sort or another by enticements from society, but Job claims he has never been guilty of letting peer pressure guide his path.

Job 31:33-34 "Have I covered my transgressions like Adam, by hiding my iniquity in my bosom, because I feared the great multitude, and the contempt of families terrified me, and kept silent and did not go out of doors?" NAS

When I first realized the impact of the following scripture, I sat in amazement that Job would ever make such a statement. Job has indicated that God is his opponent and his enemy, and he has demanded that God present His grievances against him. He now indicates God is his adversary, and he renews his request for a written indictment. Job says he will put the accusation on his head like a crown and come before God like a prince. WOW! The passage below stuns me! Read the scripture a few times to get the full impact of how Job's arrogance had put him on the edge of lunacy:

Job 31:35-37 "Oh that I had one to hear me! Behold, here is my signature; let the Almighty answer me! And the indictment which my adversary has written, surely I would carry it on my shoulder; I would bind it to myself like a crown. I would declare to Him the number of my steps; like a prince I would approach Him." NAS

In his defense before God, Job is about to rest his case; however, he ends with another hypothetical sin and its proper punishment. Job has taken care of his own land and has not violated the property of others. After these comments, the Narrator notes that Job has completed his speech.

Job 31:38-40 "If my land cries out against me, and its furrows weep together; if I have eaten its fruit without money, or have caused its owners to lose their lives, let briars grow instead of wheat, and stinkweed instead of barley." The words of Job are ended. NAS

What Job has done is to list many sins of which he claims to have had no part. He knows of others who have done these things without consequences; therefore, he concludes God has wronged him. He may be able to give a long, detailed list of sins he has not committed; however, this does not prove God to be in the wrong. Job's very comments show his arrogance and haughty nature in accusing God of being unjust. Job knows which sins deserve the appropriate punishment! With the words of Job ended, the Narrator makes one of the most important statements in the entire book.

Job 32:1 "So these three men ceased to answer Job, because he was righteous in his own eyes." NRS

Job's friends must have been absolutely speechless after this last tirade, but this last speech sets the stage for the mediator to arrive and help all concerned to see what is wrong with the picture. The next two chapters of this volume tell about Elihu, God's answer to Job's prayer for a mediator.

STUDY GUIDE – Chapter 9

1. Do you consider Job's comments to God as prayers?

2. Why does Job conclude that God will not judge him innocent?

3. If Job is flawed, is it God's fault for creating him with defects?

4. How does Job bargain with God in *Job 13:20-22*?   Have you ever bargained with God?

5. How significant is Job's reference to God as his enemy and opponent?

6. How did Job waver in his beliefs about life after death?

7. Did God actually weigh Job on dishonest scales? (*Job 31:*6)

8. Discuss Job's comments about handling God's indictment. (*Job 31:36-37*)

CHAPTER 10

– CAN ANYONE OUT THERE HELP?

Job needs a mediator to help resolve his miseries.

Throughout his dialogues, Job calls for a one-on-one conversation with God, enabling him to present his case and defend himself; this proves to be an unreasonable request. When Moses asked God to show his glory (appear before him), God responded with the following message:

> *Exodus 33:20-23 "You cannot see my face, for no one may see me and live." Then the Lord said, "There is a place near me where you may stand on a rock. When my glory passes by, I will put you in a cleft in the rock and cover you with my hand until I have passed by. Then I will remove my hand and you will see my back; but my face must not be seen." NIV*

God's infinite nature far surpasses man's finite nature, making it impossible for Job's request to be granted. This point is completed when John writes:

> *"No one has ever seen God. But if we love each other, God lives in us, and his love is brought to full expression in us." 1 John 4:12 NLT*

If it is true that no man has ever seen God, how can the scriptures be reconciled that tell of humans having a God-encounter? Because of God's omnipresence, He has chosen to take different forms for such encounters. For the human form to come into the presence of the Almighty, God has made provisions through Bible history by using hand-picked humans and by taking the form of an angel or a flesh and bone mediator.

127

The word mediator is defined in the following terms:

1. One that reconciles differences between disputants.
2. A settlement of a dispute or controversy by setting up an independent person between two contending parties in order to aid them in the settlement of their disagreement.

Because of man's weak fleshly nature, all humans come into conflict with God at various times. Because a direct God-encounter destroys flesh, the need arrives for mediation. Jesus, our mediator in today's world, has this to say:

"I am the way, the truth, and the life. No one comes to the father except through me." John 14:6 NKJV

When reality appears at times, Job understands he cannot not file suit against God and take the Almighty to task. Since humans cannot encounter the actual presence of God, a mediator is essential to aid in times of trial. At times Job realizes the need for a mediator to step in and assist him through his "alligator pond."

Job 9:32-35 "God is not a mortal like me, so I cannot argue with him or take him to trial. If only there were a mediator who could bring us together, but there is none. The mediator could make God stop beating me, and I would no longer live in terror of his punishment. Then I could speak to him without fear, but I cannot do that in my own strength." NLT

God has used many methods and has taken many forms in approaching man, but none of these have been in His original form, a form no one understands or can explain. In Genesis, when the world had become unbearably wicked, God sent a man named Noah to plead with people to change their lives. In the following passage, the apostle Peter draws the link between Noah and Jesus Christ, because God's Spirit was in Noah, just as it was present in Jesus Christ, and through that Spirit, Noah preached to those imprisoned by sin:

1 Peter 3:18-21 For Christ also suffered once for sins, the righteous for the unrighteous, to bring you to God. He was put to death in the body but made alive in the Spirit. In that

state he went and made proclamation to the imprisoned spirits to those who were disobedient long ago when God waited patiently in the days of Noah while the ark was being built. In it only a few people, eight in all, were saved through water, and this water symbolizes baptism that now saves you also—not the removal of dirt from the body but the pledge of a clear conscience toward God. It saves you by the resurrection of Jesus Christ. TNIV

In Genesis, God also appeared to Abraham in the personage of a man called Melchizedek; this occurred after Abraham's victory over a coalition of rulers that had captured his nephew Lot. Upon returning from the victory, Abraham was met by Melchizedek, king of Salem and priest of God. This was 500 years before there was a Levitical priesthood. No one would have understood the nature of this encounter if not for the writer of *Hebrews*, who revealed interesting things about Melchizedek.

Jesus is both our King and our Priest; the Melchizedek story is the first to place these two offices together. Melchizedek's arrival came 500 years before the kings of Israel and the Levitical priesthood. How could he be a priest of God since there was no earthly priesthood?

Correlate this with the theological concept that Jesus Christ is both priest and king. How could Jesus be both? Kings of the Jews came from the tribe of Judah, and priests came from the tribe of Levi. No human being could possibly be both king and priest under the Jewish system, but Jesus' mother was human and His Father was divine. Jesus' kingship could be traced to the fact that both Joseph and Mary came from the tribe of Judah. What about His priesthood? The author of *Hebrews* states that Jesus' priesthood did not come through Levi because those priests die; his priesthood came through the order of Melchizedek.

Great clues are given to Melchizedek's nature: he had no father or mother, had no genealogical background, lived an indestructible life, and held an eternal priesthood. Abraham paid tithes to Melchizedek from the plunder, proving conclusively that Melchizedek was superior to Abraham. A reading of *Hebrews 5:1-Hebrews 7:28* reveals these links to prove Melchizedek was an appearance of God in human form.

Abraham had a second encounter with God in human form. There can be no question that God appeared in the form of three men when one reads the passage below:

> *Genesis 18:1-3 Now the Lord appeared to him by the oaks of Mamre, while he was sitting at the tent door in the heat of the day. When he lifted up his eyes and looked, behold, three men were standing opposite him; and when he saw them, he ran from the tent door to meet them and bowed himself to the earth, and said, "My Lord, if now I have found favor in Your sight, please do not pass Your servant by."* NAS

When one of the men spoke to Abraham, it was God doing the speaking. God needed to give Abraham a personal message, and He did this through the three men.

> *Genesis 18:9-10 "Where is your wife Sarah?" they asked him. "There, in the tent," he said. Then the Lord said, "I will surely return to you about this time next year, and Sarah your wife will have a son."* NIV

According to the *Genesis 19* account, two of the men (who were angels) left for Sodom and Gomorrah to warn Abraham's nephew Lot. The visitor who remained with Abraham was called "the Lord."

> *Genesis 18:22 The men turned away and went toward Sodom, but Abraham remained standing before the Lord.* NIV

Abraham's grandson Jacob had a meeting with God when he stopped for the night and became involved in an all-night wrestling match. This meeting was significant because it led to God's changing Jacob's name to Israel.

> *Genesis 32:24-31 Then Jacob was left alone, and a man wrestled with him until daybreak. When he saw that he had not prevailed against him, he touched the socket of his thigh; so the socket of Jacob's thigh was dislocated while he wrestled with him. Then he said, "Let me go, for the dawn is breaking." But he said, "I will not let you go unless you bless me." So he said to him, "What is your name?" And he said, "Jacob." He said, "Your name shall no longer be*

Jacob, but Israel; for you have striven with God and with men and have prevailed." Then Jacob asked him and said, "Please tell me your name." But he said, "Why is it that you ask my name?" And he blessed him there. So Jacob named the place Peniel, for he said, "I have seen God face to face, yet my life has been preserved." NASU

Man? Angel? God? With whom did Jacob wrestle? Hosea, in writing about the event, leaves no doubt that Jacob wrestled with God in the form of an angel or man.

Hosea 12:4-5 He strove with the angel and prevailed, he wept and sought his favor; he met him at Bethel, and there he spoke with him. The Lord the God of hosts, the Lord is his name! NRS

To see God's face would have resulted in Jacob's death, so God appeared as an angel in the form of a man. A personal encounter was needed to accomplish the task of changing Jacob's name to Israel. God sent a mediator to get Jacob's attention and complete the mission.

The latter part of the book of *Genesis* details the life of Joseph, a son of Jacob/Israel, in a beautiful parallel of Jesus Christ. He was sold for silver into slavery just as Jesus was sold for silver to become sin for the world. In Egypt, Joseph was treated as a criminal and placed in a prison with the king's cupbearer and baker. About 1800 years later, Jesus was nailed to a cross between two thieves. Joseph made provisions for his family as they lived in a foreign land, just as Jesus provides for His family as they live in a land not their own. Joseph died in Egypt, but he left orders for his bones to be moved to the Promised Land, because he knew God would deliver His people. Jesus died in Jerusalem, but He rose from the dead and ascended into heaven. God sometimes mediates by taking human form, and He sometimes mediates by empowering a human to accomplish the task.

Moses' first encounter with the Lord occurred through an angel speaking out of a burning bush that was not being consumed by the fire. When the Angel spoke, it was God speaking to Moses.

Exodus 3:4-5 When the Lord saw that he had caught Moses' attention, God called to him from the bush, "Moses! Moses!" "Here I am!" Moses replied. "Do not come any

closer," God told him. "Take off your sandals, for you are standing on holy ground." RSV

Between the time that Moses broke the two tablets containing the Ten Commandments and the meeting with God to get the new tables of stone, Moses had frequent communications with God. *Exodus 33* relates how Moses would set up a tent outside the camp to meet with God, and as he entered the tent, the pillar of cloud would descend, signaling the presence of God in a form posing no danger to Moses.

> *Exodus 33:9-11 As Moses went into the tent, the pillar of cloud would come down and stay at the entrance, while the Lord spoke with Moses. Whenever the people saw the pillar of cloud standing at the entrance to the tent, they all stood and worshiped, each at the entrance to his tent. The Lord would speak to Moses face to face, as a man speaks with his friend. NIV*

Hold the phone! Earlier we learned from *Exodus 33* that no one could see the face of God and live; in the same chapter we learn that Moses spoke "face-to-face" with God. This is a figure of speech indicating the intimate conversations between Moses and the Lord; there is no contradiction in *Exodus 33*. When Moses was on Mount Sinai the second time, God allowed him to see His back, but never His face because God wanted to keep his servant alive.

Moses had a mediator in the form of the Burning Bush and in the form of the Pillar of Cloud, but we must realize that Moses also became a mediator between Israel and God. The Israelites realized their need for a buffer zone after they heard the powerful sound of God's voice speaking the Ten Commandments from Mount Sinai.

> *Exodus 20:18-19 Now all the people witnessed the thunderings, the lightning flashes, the sound of the trumpet, and the mountain smoking; and when the people saw it, they trembled and stood afar off. Then they said to Moses, "You speak with us, and we will hear; but let not God speak with us, lest we die." NKJV*

Moses, through his writing of the Pentateuch, served as a mediator in introducing the greatest mediator of all, Jesus Christ. He did this in writing pictures and parallels of Jesus in stories about Noah, Melchizedek, Abraham, Jacob, and Joseph. No wonder Jesus made the following claim about Moses:

> *John 5:4-5 "For if you believed Moses, you would believe me; for he wrote of me. But if you do not believe his writings, how will you believe my words?"* NCV

In addition to God's mediators spoken of by Moses, the book of *Joshua* tells of an encounter with a heavenly being. After Moses' death, Joshua was made leader of Israel, but one day he saw someone he realized did not have a normal human appearance.

> *Joshua 5:13-15 Joshua was near Jericho when he looked up and saw a man standing in front of him with a sword in his hand. Joshua went to him and asked, "Are you a friend or an enemy?" The man answered, "I am neither. I have come as the commander of the Lord's army." Then Joshua bowed facedown on the ground and asked, "Does my master have a command for me, his servant?" The commander of the LORD's army answered, "Take off your sandals, because the place where you are standing is holy." So Joshua did.* NCV

These examples should suffice to establish the point that all humans need mediation in approaching God. Job is absolutely aware that God is bigger than himself, but he is frustrated that he cannot have his day in God's court. He complains about God's keeping His whereabouts a secret, or perhaps He is hiding. Job indicates he wants a face-to-face meeting with his Judge. Perhaps he knows nothing about the prohibition of seeing the face of God.

If it were not possible to see God face-to-face without certain death, Job would at least like to have somebody stand up for him. Job pleads with his friends to believe in his innocence, and he seeks their support before God. In seeking sympathy and support, he tells of his desire to have someone write about his misery.

> *Job 19:23-24 "Oh, that my words were recorded, that they were written on a scroll, that they were inscribed with an iron tool on lead, or engraved in rock forever!"* NIV

The options Job has considered for relief seem rather clear; 1) A direct meeting with God to defend himself. In today's world there is a saying that a man who defends himself in court has a fool for a lawyer. What does this say about Job's desire to present his own case? 2) Job considers the possibility of asking for mercy, but he never humbles himself to this level. 3) He could use a mediator; Job did not realize at that time that God would supply a mediator to prepare the way for his relief.

The text is not clear concerning Elihu's arrival. Was he there from the beginning of the fray, refraining from comment until he perceived the moment was right? Perhaps, but why did the Narrator not tell us about his presence until *Job 32*? Is it possible Elihu's intricate knowledge of the dialogues between Job and his friends was given him from God? Just as God guided other humans such as Noah, Moses, and Joseph, God could have blessed Elihu with a "recording" of the event. This would explain why Elihu could say, "You now have one with you who is perfect in knowledge." He is not being a smart aleck, bragging about his personal intelligence; rather, he is referring to the presence of God's perfect knowledge coming through him.

ELIHU IS THE MEDIATOR BETWEEN JOB AND GOD

When Elihu begins speaking (in *Job 32 – 37)*, all other communication ceases. Elihu even encourages Job to speak up if he has something to say, but nothing comes from Job's mouth. I can see silence prevailing because Job and his friends are stunned that Elihu knows all about the conversations, word-for-word. What does the Narrator have to say about Elihu?

> *Job 32:1-5 So these three men stopped answering Job, because he was righteous in his own eyes. But Elihu son of Barakel the Buzite, of the family of Ram, became very angry with Job for justifying himself rather than God. He was also angry with the three friends, because they had found no way to refute Job, and yet had condemned him. Now Elihu had waited before speaking to Job because they were older than he. But when he saw that the three men had nothing more to say, his anger was aroused. TNIV*

From what the Narrator reveals, we know Elihu is not a heavenly being such as Melchizedek who appeared to Abraham, or the man who wrestled with Jacob, or the Commander of the Lord's army who appeared to Joshua. Elihu has a genealogical record; he is absolute flesh and bones. We also know Elihu's anger was aroused because of Job's arrogance and because Job's three friends have falsely accused a God-fearing innocent man. Elihu's message is on the same track with the message of God when He arrives to address Job. Elihu prepares the way for God's arrival.

After the Narrator gives readers a brief glimpse of Elihu's family background, his next comments reveal that Elihu is much younger than Job and his friends. He states that he has refrained from speaking, deferring to those older than himself.

> *Job 32:6-10 Elihu son of Barachel the Buzite answered: "I am young in years, and you are aged; therefore I was timid and afraid to declare my opinion to you. I said, 'Let days speak, and many years teach wisdom.'"* NRS

Something causes Elihu to set his fear aside and give his insights into the prevailing mistaken concepts. In the passage below, Elihu states that he broke his silence because the Spirit of God drove him to speak. The Spirit of God is where understanding resides, not in the age of a person. God chose to send His Spirit into Elihu to mediate in His behalf.

> *Job 32:8 10 "But truly it is the spirit in a mortal, the breath of the Almighty, that makes for understanding. It is not the old that are wise, nor the aged that understand what is right. Therefore I say, 'Listen to me; let me also declare my opinion.'"* NRS

Job and his friends have relied on their own experiences to support their arguments. But Elihu's claim gains immediate attention and much credibility; in the passage above he says, "I speak because the Spirit within me will not allow me to remain silent." Elihu continues by chastising the friends for their accusations and for their wild assertions about Job. God condemns the friends for the same thing in *Job 38-41*. Elihu says he will not be relying on the same line of reasoning Job's friends have attempted.

> *Job 32:11-14 "I hung on your words while you spoke; I listened carefully to your arguments. While you searched*

for the right words, I was all ears. And now what have you proved? Nothing. Nothing you say has even touched Job. And don't excuse yourselves by saying, 'We've done our best. Now it's up to God to talk sense into him.' Job has yet to contend with me. And rest assured, I won't be using your arguments"! TM

Job and his friends are apparently stunned to silence as they listen to Elihu, but this does not slow Elihu down because the Spirit of God is compelling him to speak. Elihu knows his message must be delivered accurately because "his Maker" will punish him if he fails in what he says to Job and his friends. Elihu is full of opinions and about to burst, but the Spirit holds him to the task of preparing his listeners for the arrival of God.

Job 32:15-22 "They are dismayed, they no longer answer; words have failed them. Shall I wait, because they do not speak, because they stop and no longer answer? I too will answer my share; I also will tell my opinion. For I am full of words; the spirit within me constrains me. Behold, my belly is like unvented wine; like new wineskins it is about to burst. Let me speak that I may get relief; let me open my lips and answer. Let me now be partial to no one, nor flatter any man. For I do not know how to flatter, else my Maker would soon take me away." NASU

To get Job's attention and to tweak his desire to hear his message, Elihu claims the following:

- What I say will be the truth.
- The Spirit of God is behind my message.
- I am the mediator you have been requesting!
- Feel free to speak up if you believe you have an answer to what I am saying.
- I am totally human; we're all made of clay.

Elihu's statement that he is made of clay seems to be a "no-brainer." However, he is aware that his message could be considered as coming through a supernatural being. Elihu will be speaking through God's inspiration, but he is as human as those whom he addresses. Observe Elihu's points in the following passage:

Job 33:1-7 "Please listen, Job, to what I have to say. I have begun to speak; now let me continue. I will speak the truth with all sincerity, for the Spirit of God has made me, and the breath of the Almighty gives me life. Don't hesitate to answer me if you can. Look, I am the one you were wishing for, someone to stand between you and God and to be both his representative and yours. You need not be frightened of me. I am not some person of renown to make you nervous and afraid. I, too, am made of common clay." LB

In the passage above Elihu refers to his being the one Job had wished for; Elihu claims to be Job's spokesperson before God. This, in plain terms, is the definition for a mediator. Some versions make it quite clear that Elihu is God's answer to Job's prayer for a mediator.

Job 33:6 "Truly I am as your spokesman before God; I also have been formed out of clay. NKJV

Job 33:6 "Behold, I [am] according to thy wish in God's stead: I also am formed out of the clay." WB

Elihu has more to say about his role as God's messenger. Because of the importance of Elihu's message, more than one version will be presented to establish Elihu's credibility. He will claim the following credentials:

- I speak in God's behalf.
- My message comes from afar.
- God has endowed me with perfect knowledge for this occasion. (Elihu is not referring to himself as being "perfect in knowledge.")
- I guarantee my message to be true.

Read the following versions carefully to discern the impact of Elihu's comments:

Job 36:2-4 "Bear with me a little, and I will show you that there are yet words to speak on God's behalf. I will fetch my knowledge from afar; I will ascribe righteousness to my Maker. For truly my words are not false; One who is perfect in knowledge is with you." NKJV

137

Job 36:2-4 "Bear with me a little longer and I will show you that there is more to be said in God's behalf. I get my knowledge from afar; I will ascribe justice to my Maker. Be assured that my words are not false; one perfect in knowledge is with you." NIV

Job 36:2-4 "Stay with me a little longer. I'll convince you. There's still more to be said on God's side. I learned all this firsthand from the Source; everything I know about justice I owe to my Maker himself. Trust me, I'm giving you undiluted truth; believe me, I know these things inside and out." TM

Job 36:2-4 "Bear with me a little, and I will show you, for I have yet something to say on God's behalf. I will bring my knowledge from far away, and ascribe righteousness to my Maker. For truly my words are not false; one who is perfect in knowledge is with you." NRS

Job 36:2-4 "Give me a little more time, and I will make it clear to you; for I have still something to say for God. I will get my knowledge from far, and I will give righteousness to my Maker. For truly my words are not false; one who has all knowledge is talking with you." BBE

If Elihu's claims are false, what he has said is absolute blasphemy; however, when God appears in *Job 38-41*, He chastises Job and his three friends, but God has nothing to say to Elihu.

When all the data is gathered concerning Elihu, the following information can be discerned from the scriptures we have examined:

- God sends Elihu in response to Job's desire for a mediator.
- Elihu is as human as Job, but God has endowed him with perfect knowledge.
- Elihu's words, given from God, are absolute truth.
- Elihu is speaking in God's behalf.

In addition to the above points, consider the following:

- Neither Job nor his friends ever respond or deny what Elihu says.

138

- God does not correct Elihu; therefore, everything he says stands as true.
- Elihu will tell Job the very same things God has to say.
- Elihu introduces Job to the Almighty by describing the approaching thunder and lightning.

As Elihu continues speaking in *Job 36*, he sees a storm approaching and knows that God is on His way to speak to Job. He has been talking about the greatness of God, but now his message shifts to the sight of lightning and the sound of thunder. As his description of the coming storm builds toward the event, he calls on Job to observe God in action.

> *Job 36:26-33 "Behold, God is great, and we do not know Him; nor can the number of His years be discovered. For He draws up drops of water, which distill as rain from the mist, which the clouds drop down and pour abundantly on man. Indeed, can anyone understand the spreading of clouds, the thunder from His canopy? Look, He scatters his light upon it, and covers the depths of the sea. For by these He judges the peoples; He gives food in abundance. He covers His hands with lightning, and commands it to strike. His thunder declares it, the cattle also, concerning the rising storm."* NKJV

God has sent Elihu on a mission to assist Job in his struggles through suffering; notice in the following verses how excited Elihu becomes when he sees the approaching storm. Elihu is completing his role as mediator, and now it is Job's turn to hear the Lord through the storm; furthermore, Elihu serves as the conduit between Job and God. He is introducing Job to the One he has been demanding to meet in court for a hearing.

> *Job 37:1-5 "At this my heart pounds and leaps from its place. Listen! Listen to the roar of his voice, to the rumbling that comes from his mouth. He unleashes his lightning beneath the whole heaven and sends it to the ends of the earth. After that comes the sound of his roar; he thunders with his majestic voice. When his voice resounds, he holds nothing back. God's voice thunders in marvelous ways; he does great things beyond our understanding."* NIV

When I hear God's thunder, I often think of Job and the approaching storm. Elihu spends a little time explaining God's control over nature and the blessings of rain, but he explains that rain can also be sent to punish. All nature responds when God is at work with the storms of life; God does these things to make His presence known.

> *Job 37:6-13 "For to the snow he says, 'Fall on the earth'; and the shower of rain, his heavy shower of rain, serves as a sign on everyone's hand, so that all whom he has made may know it. Then the animals go into their lairs and remain in their dens. From its chamber comes the whirlwind, and cold from the scattering winds. By the breath of God ice is given, and the broad waters are frozen fast. He loads the thick cloud with moisture; the clouds scatter his lightning. They turn round and round by his guidance, to accomplish all that he commands them on the face of the habitable world. Whether for correction, or for his land, or for love, he causes it to happen." NRS*

Once again, Elihu calls on Job to listen to the power of God. Job has been demanding that God listen to the case he has prepared. Elihu explains that Job is not on the same plane with God, the same theme God will use when He arrives in the storm to speak to Job. Job cannot do the things God can do, and he does not know the things God knows; simply put, Job is not God. As the storm continues its approach, Elihu criticizes Job for his demands upon the Almighty.

> *Job 37:14-20 "Job, listen to this: Stop and notice God's miracles. Do you know how God controls the clouds and makes his lightning flash? Do you know how the clouds hang in the sky? Do you know the miracles of God, who knows everything? You suffer in your clothes when the land is silenced by the hot, south wind. You cannot stretch out the sky like God and make it look as hard as polished bronze. Tell us what we should say to him; we cannot get our arguments ready because we do not have enough understanding. Should God be told that I want to speak? Would a person ask to be swallowed up?" NCV*

As Elihu completes the introduction of God to Job, he reminds Job that one cannot see the actual presence of God; God's nature is too awesome. Job has been demanding something that would ultimately destroy him if his request were granted.

> *Job 37:21-24 "We cannot look at the sun, for it shines brightly in the sky when the wind clears away the clouds. So also, golden splendor comes from the mountain of God. He is clothed in dazzling splendor. We cannot imagine the power of the Almighty; but even though he is just and righteous, he does not destroy us. No wonder people everywhere fear him. All who are wise show him reverence."* NLT

The preparation has been made, and it is time for God to enter the scene through the storm, a death-preventing method in which He can speak to Job. A bit of clarification needs to take place concerning God's opening comment. God's speech to Job will be analyzed in chapter 12 of this volume, but for the time-being, notice that God is speaking to Job about his degrading comments made to and about the Almighty:

> *Job 38:1-2 Then the Lord answered Job out of the whirlwind, and said: "Who is this who darkens counsel by words without knowledge?"* NKJV

God is not asking Job about Elihu's presence and comments; He is speaking directly to Job, and Job knows it. God never corrects Elihu for any part of his speech to Job. When Job steps toward the stage of Acceptance, he admits the error of his way.

> *Job 42:3 "You asked, 'Who is this who hides counsel without knowledge?' Therefore I have uttered what I did not understand, things too wonderful for me, which I did not know".* NKJV

With the evidence presented in this chapter, it hopefully is clear that God has sent Elihu to prepare the way for His confrontation with Job. The next chapter analyzes Elihu's message as he cushions Job for his encounter with the Almighty.

STUDY GUIDE – Chapter 10

1. Why does God use mediators to work with mankind?

2. What evidence indicates that Melchizedek was a God-encounter with Abraham?

3. Was Jacob correct in saying he had seen God face-to-face and lived?

4. Why did the Israelites ask Moses to be their mediator?

5. How did God appear to Joshua as a mediator?

6. What evidence indicates that Elihu was a mediator sent from God?

7. Why do Job and friends remain silent during Elihu's entire speech?

8. Discuss Elihu's excitement as he sees God approaching in the storm.

CHAPTER 11

– I'M READY TO HEAR THE MEDIATOR

Elihu prepares Job for his encounter with God.

Having established the importance of the words of Elihu, it is now time to seek understanding of his message to Job and his three friends. Elihu's audience may have included others passing by, but his focus is on four men who must be amazed upon hearing his comments. If he had been there the entire time, they would have been impressed with his memory of the conversations; on the other hand, if he had just arrived knowing everything that had taken place, I believe they must have been totally stunned.

Elihu has claimed that he knows every word that has been uttered, and he backs this up by quoting comments made early in the verbal exchange. When someone's words are recorded and he listens to the exact words he or she has uttered, it is often a sobering moment. Of course, recorders did not exist at that time, so rule out that possibility. However, Elihu must have astounded Job by repeating his own comments, and Job's amazement would have been even greater if Elihu had just appeared on the scene with this kind of knowledge.

> *Job 33:8-12 "Surely, you have spoken in my hearing, and I have heard the sound of your words. You say, 'I am clean, without transgression; I am pure, and there is no iniquity in me. Look, he finds occasions against me, he counts me as his enemy; he puts my feet in the stocks, and watches all my paths.' But in this you are not right. I will answer you: God is greater than any mortal."* NRS

Elihu questions Job concerning his complaint that God has not spoken to him. He explains to Job that God does speak to people; one way it occurs is through dreams. In the passage below, one key verse stands out big—God speaks to people in dreams or visions to keep them from pride. In this statement, Elihu actually identifies the cause of Job's suffering—arrogance! God later identifies pride as the major issue when He arrives in the storm to speak with Job in *Job 38*.

> *Job 33:13-18   "Why do you complain to him that he responds to no one's words? For God does speak—now one way, now another—though no one perceives it. In a dream, in a vision of the night, when deep sleep falls on people as they slumber in their beds, he may speak in their ears and terrify them with warnings, to turn them from wrongdoing and keep them from pride, to preserve them from the pit, their lives from perishing by the sword."* TNIV

Elihu further explains that God communicates to people through suffering; it has been apparent that Job has not appreciated God's use of this method of communication. Job's experiences correlate so closely with the message of the author of *Hebrews*.

> *Hebrews 12:4-10   In your struggle against sin you have not yet resisted to the point of shedding your blood.   And you have forgotten the exhortation that addresses you as children—"My child, do not regard lightly the discipline of the Lord, or lose heart when you are punished by him; for the Lord disciplines those whom he loves, and chastises every child whom he accepts." Endure trials for the sake of discipline. God is treating you as children; for what child is there whom a parent does not discipline? If you do not have that discipline in which all children share, then you are illegitimate and not his children. Moreover, we had human parents to discipline us, and we respected them. Should we not be even more willing to be subject to the Father of spirits and live? For they disciplined us for a short time as seemed best to them, but he disciplines us for our good, in order that we may share his holiness.* NRS

Elihu gives a description of a suffering man who has encountered similar circumstances to those afflicting Job. God at times takes people to the brink of death in an effort to guide their spiritual walk. Read carefully as Elihu describes God's communication through suffering:

Job 33:19-22 "People may be corrected while in bed in great pain; they may have continual pain in their very bones. They may be in such pain that they even hate food, even the very best meal. Their body becomes so thin there is almost nothing left of it, and their bones that were hidden now stick out. They are near death, and their life is almost over." NCV

It has been very clear that Job has not recognized God's communication through his suffering to be in his best interest, and his rebellious words have prevented blessings to come through his ordeal. However, all is not futile. Elihu explains that an angel, a mediator, can come to his aid. The word <u>angel</u> simply means "messenger from God." As pointed out in the previous chapter, the messenger may be a heavenly creature, or the messenger may be a person empowered by God for a special task. The word <u>mediator</u> should catch our attention. Elihu has already said that he is the one for whom Job has been wishing. Elihu's purpose in speaking is to prepare Job for his encounter with God. Both God and his messenger, Elihu, are interested in Job's soul. It is a hard pill for Job to swallow, but his suffering results from God's love for his child. This message is found in the works of Solomon:

Proverbs 3:11-12 My son, do not despise the Lord's discipline and do not resent his rebuke, because the Lord disciplines those he loves, as a father the son he delights in. NIV

It is interesting that the writer of *Hebrews12:5-6,* quotes the *Proverbs* passage above in making his point about God's purpose in suffering The author further claims that those who learn from their suffering and adjust their lives in accordance with the will of God have a rich harvest awaiting them.

Hebrews 12:11 Now, discipline always seems painful rather than pleasant at the time, but later it yields the peaceful fruit of righteousness to those who have been trained by it. RSV

If Job learns and is trained by his suffering, a great harvest awaits him, and this certainly turns out to be the case. However, Elihu lets Job know he is in need of mediation and intercessory prayer. Elihu is doing his best to assist Job, but Job needs to do some praying of his own.

Job 33:23-26 "Yet if there is an angel on his side as a mediator, one out of a thousand, to tell a man what is right for him, to be gracious to him and say, 'Spare him from going down to the pit; I have found a ransom for him'— then his flesh is renewed like a child's; it is restored as in the days of his youth. He prays to God and finds favor with him, he sees God's face and shouts for joy; he is restored by God to his righteous state." NIV

Elihu has done well in explaining God's attempts to assist Job in his suffering; he even tells Job how he needs to confess. The hymn to which he refers in the passage below is an admission that God has done less than Job deserved. All sin is punishable by eternal damnation; Job is still alive and has a chance to reverse his circumstances. The Lord had protected Job from death by the limits He had placed on Satan. As the author of Hebrews said, "You have not suffered to the point of shedding your blood." Basically, what Elihu has said in the hymn below is—"You are right, Job; you have not received what you deserve. God could have just sent you to hell with your arrogance, but He loved you so much that He sent you pain and suffering because He wants your heart." The bottom line is that suffering is intended to put humans in their proper place. Relationships with God are developed through pain and suffering! In the following passage, Elihu continues his instructions to Job concerning what the suffering person should do to reverse the situation. God's purpose for his calamities was to prepare Job for his future life, just as God prepares His followers today for eternal blessings.

Job 33:26-30 "He will pray to God who has restored him to favor, and will come into his presence with joy. He will tell others how he has received saving justice and sing this hymn before his companions, 'I sinned and left the path of right, but God has not punished me as my sin deserved. He has spared my soul from going down to the abyss and is making my life see the light.' All this is what God keeps doing again and yet again for human beings, to snatch souls back from the abyss and to make the light of the living still shine." NJB

Elihu has more to say before he invites Job to speak up; but he does call upon all to evaluate and judge his comments. In the following passage, he also tells Job his desire and goal is to exonerate him by sharing words of wisdom. That certainly describes the role of a mediator who is working to resolve conflict. There is no way Elihu could exonerate Job if he were not a messenger sent from God.

> *Job 33:31-34:4 "Pay attention, O Job, listen to me; keep silent, and let me speak. Then if you have anything to say, answer me; speak, for I desire to justify you. If not, listen to me; keep silent, and I will teach you wisdom."* NASU

Once again, Elihu directs his message to the three friends; he leaves the door open for all within hearing distance to comment on his thoughts. Just as the friends have listened to What Elihu has had to say to Job, Job hears what he says to Eliphaz, Bildad, and Zophar.

> *Job 34:1-4 Elihu further answered and said: "Hear my words, you wise men; give ear to me, you who have knowledge. For the ear tests words as the palate tastes food. Let us choose justice for ourselves; let us know among ourselves what is good."* NKJV

As Elihu continues his dialogue, he once again replays Job's words spoken in Anger, and Job must reflect on what he has said. Job has actually said it doesn't pay to serve God if the end result is suffering. Elihu questions the three friends in an effort to generate thought on the part of all concerned, but he doesn't supply answers at this point. What a reminder when Elihu quotes Job as claiming, "It doesn't pay to try to please God!"

> *Job 34:5-9 "We've all heard Job say, 'I'm in the right, but God won't give me a fair trial. When I defend myself, I'm called a liar to my face. I've done nothing wrong, and I get punished anyway.' Have you ever heard anything to beat this? Does nothing faze this man Job? Do you think he's spent too much time in bad company, hanging out with the wrong crowd, so that now he's parroting their line: 'It doesn't pay to try to please God'?"* TM

Elihu claims to be speaking through God's Spirit; remember that we learned in *Job 36*, discussed in the previous chapter of this volume, that Elihu claimed to be speaking on God's behalf. In accomplishing this task, Elihu defends God's behavior and His judgment of those who rule on the earth. God is over all, and no one put Him in charge of anything, and no one created Him. He has created all beings, and He has the right to judge over them. Elihu demands that God dispenses justice in His decisions.

> *Job 34:10-20   "So listen to me, you who can understand. God can never do wrong! It is impossible for the Almighty to do evil. God pays people back for what they have done and gives them what their actions deserve. Truly God will never do wrong; the Almighty will never twist what is right. No one chose God to rule over the earth or put him in charge of the whole world. If God should decide to take away life and breath, then everyone would die together and turn back into dust. If you can understand, hear this; listen to what I have to say. Can anyone govern who hates what is right?   How can you blame God who is both fair and powerful?   God is the one who says to kings, 'You are worthless,' or to important people, 'You are evil.' He is not nicer to princes than other people, nor kinder to rich people than poor people, because he made them all with his own hands. They can die in a moment, in the middle of the night. They are struck down, and then they pass away; powerful people die without help. NCV*

Elihu praises God's Omnipresence and Omnipotence in the next section of his speech. God is everywhere and knows all things; therefore, it is senseless to call God to question for what is taking place. When the Narrator first spoke about Job's character, he was stating truth; compared to other persons, Job was a jewel of a human being. However, Job was human; he was not God, nor could he ever compete with God's nature. Job's gifts to the poor could never equal what God supplies to those in need. God does not ask man for permission to perform whatever He decides to do, and everything He does is to protect nations and people from being harmed by evil. Elihu presents these thoughts below:

> *Job 34:21-30   "His eyes are on the ways of men; he sees their every step. There is no dark place, no deep shadow, where evildoers can hide. God has no need to examine men further that they should come before him for judgment. Without inquiry he shatters the mighty and sets up others in their place.   Because he takes note of their deeds, he*

148

overthrows them in the night and they are crushed. He punishes them for their wickedness where everyone can see them, because they turned from following him and had no regard for any of his ways. They caused the cry of the poor to come before him, so that he heard the cry of the needy. But if he remains silent, who can condemn him? If he hides his face, who can see him? Yet he is over man and nation alike, to keep a godless man from ruling, from laying snares for the people. NIV

Elihu presents Job with two options given to all individuals: A person can admit he has erred and dedicate himself to making necessary changes, or a person can continue on the same path. He gives Job another invitation to comment on which person God should reward.

Job 34:31-33 "But suppose someone says to God, 'I am guilty, but I will not sin anymore. Teach me what I cannot see. If I have done wrong, I will not do it again.' So, Job, should God reward you as you want when you refuse to change? You must decide, not I, so tell me what you know." NCV

In his mediator role, Elihu informs Job that whatever wedge has been driven between him and his God, he is adding to the problem with his false accusations about and against the Almighty.

Job 34:34-37 "Men of understanding declare, wise men who hear me say to me, 'Job speaks without knowledge; his words lack insight.' Oh, that Job might be tested to the utmost for answering like a wicked man! To his sin he adds rebellion; scornfully he claps his hands among us and multiplies his words against God." TNIV

Everyone has heard Job's complaint that his righteous living had not profited him. They have also heard him question why anyone should live an upright life when it seems to do no good.

Job 35:1-3 Then Elihu said: "Do you think it is right for you to claim, 'I am righteous before God'? For you also ask, 'What's in it for me? What's the use of living a righteous life?'" NLT

149

Eliphaz, Bildad, Zophar, and Job have all attempted addressing the issues at hand, but no one has considered what effect humans have on God. God is not dependent upon man for anything, for He is far above His creation; no one can harm Him, and no one can supply God with His needs. Elihu explains that mankind's sins and good deeds affect only the person and those around him. However, God and the universe are not affected by human activity; the two are on separate planes.

> *Job 35:4-8 "I will answer you and all your friends, too. Look up into the sky, and see the clouds high above you. If you sin, how does that affect God? Even if you sin again and again, what effect will it have on him? If you are good, is this some great gift to him? What could you possibly give him? No, your sins affect only people like yourself, and your good deeds also affect only humans."* NLT

The passage below supplies one of the most important keys to understanding Job's suffering. Most people cry for mercy when they run aground; however, Job has taken a different course. He is not one to get on his knees and beg for relief; rather, he goes on the attack and accuses God of wrong doing. Elihu tells Job that God does not answer people who are filled with pride. Elihu has been pointing to this throughout his speeches; however, realizing Job and his friends are not comprehending, he explicitly puts the issue on the table: Arrogance is Job's problem!

> *Job 35:9-12 "People cry out when they are in trouble; they beg for relief from powerful people. But no one asks, 'Where is God, my Maker, who gives us songs in the night, who makes us smarter than the animals of the earth and wiser than the birds of the air?' God does not answer evil people when they cry out, because the wicked are proud."* NCV

As he did earlier in his comments to Job, Elihu once again replays Job's message to the four listeners. When many of Job's complaints are listed together, it had to have a profound and sobering effect. Job had said the following:

- I have something to say to You, but I cannot see You!
- I have a case prepared that needs Your attention!
- I'm having to wait too long for You to respond?

- You should be punishing evil people!
- I don't think You are even aware of evil!

Job's suffering was not caused by a sinful life style; his suffering came because of his pride-filled belief that his righteous life had placed him on God's level. Elihu explains to Job that his attitude and conversations were absolutely out-of-bounds. With these thoughts in mind, examine the following passage:

> *Job 35:13-16 "God does not listen to their useless begging; the Almighty pays no attention to them. He will listen to you even less when you say that you do not see him, that your case is before him, that you must wait for him, that his anger never punishes, and that he doesn't notice evil. So Job is only speaking nonsense, saying many words without knowing what is true."* NCV

As *Job 36* opens, Elihu affirms that he is speaking in God's behalf and that his words have been guided by the Almighty. Consequently, Elihu gives an absolute guarantee that he speaks the truth as God would have it spoken. Elihu's comment that Job has "one with him who is perfect in knowledge," has two possible meanings. On one hand Elihu could be viewed as the most arrogant person in the group, bragging about himself. On the other hand, it can be interpreted as referring to God's message through his servant. Since God never corrected Elihu, I believe it is evident that Elihu was speaking about God's presence, not his own. After Elihu's reaffirmation of his credibility, he continues his message.

> *Job 36:5-9 "God is almighty and yet does not despise anyone! And he is perfect in his understanding. He does not reward the wicked with his blessings, but gives them their full share of punishment. He does not ignore the good men but honors them by placing them upon eternal, kingly thrones. If troubles come upon them and they are enslaved and afflicted, then he takes the trouble to point out to them the reason, what they have done that is wrong, or how they have behaved proudly."* TLB

What are Job's options in coping with his afflictions? Elihu explains that God desires a change in Job's heart. Job is not a godless person, but he is godless in attitude because he thinks he is on God's level. Those who are godless in heart have difficulty in crying for help because crying for help is a call for mercy. Job does not see the need for mercy since he is right in his own eyes. He demands justice; furthermore, he wants his justice now! So far, Job has rejected the cry for mercy route, so what happens to those who refuse to change their hearts? They perish in their pride. The verses below end with a very revealing comment—God communicates with people through their suffering; this thought becomes very important as Elihu's message continues.

> *Job 36:10-15 "He makes them listen to correction and commands them to repent of their evil. If they obey and serve him, they will spend the rest of their days in prosperity and their years in contentment. But if they do not listen, they will perish by the sword and die without knowledge. The godless in heart harbor resentment; even when he fetters them, they do not cry for help. They die in their youth, among male prostitutes of the shrines. But those who suffer he delivers in their suffering; he speaks to them in their affliction."* NLT

Having laid the groundwork for Job to begin grasping the cause of his suffering, Elihu explains that Job's suffering had taken place in God's attempt to draw him near to Himself. God had great plans in mind for Job, but he was missing God's message; rather than evaluating what he needed to do, he had focused on whether those less godly than he were getting their due. Elihu reminds him that justice is God's business, not Job's, and that God takes care of His business. Job was declared faultless in chapters 1 and 2 of the book of *Job*, but he was on the edge of letting his wealth and power corrupt him. Wealth and power often lead to arrogance and the desire to have even more wealth and power; this, in turn, leads the seeker to use any means possible to achieve the goal. God was giving Job the opportunity to turn from this temptation; his suffering was God's way of keeping him from a life of evil.

> *Job 36:16-21 "God is leading you away from danger, Job, to a place free from distress. He is setting your table with the best food. But you are obsessed with whether the godless will be judged. Don't worry, judgment and justice will be*

upheld. But watch out, or you may be seduced by wealth.
Don't let yourself be bribed into sin. Could all your wealth
or all your mighty efforts keep you from distress? Do not
long for the cover of night, for that is when people will be
destroyed. Be on guard! Turn back from evil, for God sent
this suffering to keep you from a life of evil. NLT

What a wonderful message to all readers! When "alligator ponds" emerge, we should turn our focus to how to best serve the Lord from where we find ourselves. Resenting the "alligator pond" and examining others who have no alligators to face have no effect on altering the plight of the one who is suffering.

Job has been given the two big puzzle pieces he needs: 1) His problem stems from pride, and 2) his suffering has been God's attempt to hold his pride in check to keep him from a path of evil. With these answers supplied by Elihu's mediation, Job is on the way to being prepared for his meeting with God. The remainder of Elihu's message points to the coming whirlwind, lightning, and thunder that were signaling the arrival of God. From *Job 36:22-Job 37:13*, Elihu creates a "drum-roll approach" when he sees the approaching whirlwind and thunderstorm.

Toward the end of his description, Elihu, speaking on behalf of God, makes his last effort to prepare Job for the encounter. He asks Job questions similar to ones God will also ask concerning his ability to perform God's wonders. Throughout the following verses, Elihu contrasts the power of God to the humanity of Job. He lets Job know it is impossible to create a case to present to God because people are on the human plane, leaving them in a fog; however, when the fog clears and darkness is removed, truth becomes evident. Job should not have been demanding an immediate audience with the Almighty. As Elihu sees the approaching storm, and knowing God's arrival in the storm is imminent, he glorifies God as he introduces Job to his Creator.

Job 37:14-24 "Listen to this, O Job, stand and consider the
wonders of God. Do you know how God establishes them,
and makes the lightning of His cloud to shine? Do you know
about the layers of the thick clouds, the wonders of one
perfect in knowledge, you whose garments are hot when the
land is still because of the south wind? Can you, with Him,

spread out the skies, strong as a molten mirror? Teach us what we shall say to Him; we cannot arrange our case because of darkness. Shall it be told Him that I would speak? Or should a man say that he would be swallowed up? Now men do not see the light which is bright in the skies; but the wind has passed and cleared them. Out of the north comes golden splendor; around God is awesome majesty. The Almighty — we cannot find Him; He is exalted in power, and He will not do violence to justice and abundant righteousness. Therefore men fear Him; He does not regard any who are wise of heart." NASU:

The next voice Job hears comes out of the storm—it is the voice of God!

STUDY GUIDE – Chapter 11

1. What is the effect on Job and his friends when Elihu repeats Job's words?

2. According to Elihu, how does God speak to people?

3. Explain the difference between punishment and discipline.

4. What steps does Elihu encourage Job to take to reverse his circumstances?

5. How does Elihu deal with Job's claim that it doesn't pay to serve God?

6. Identify statements in which Elihu speaks on God's behalf.

7. Identify statements Elihu repeats that have been made by Job.

8. Describe Elihu's excitement as he sees God approaching in the storm.

CHAPTER 12

– SPEAK LORD, I'M LISTENING

By the time God arrives in a whirlwind, accompanied by thunder and lightning, Job and his three friends have expended great effort analyzing and dissecting God and His purposes for events such as those Job has experienced. The efforts of Eliphaz, Bildad, and Zophar have fallen on deaf ears, and Job has failed to move his friends to accept his conclusions. He has insisted on his innocence, and he has accused God of wrong-doing; furthermore, Job has demanded that his case be heard by the Almighty. Finally, Elihu introduces himself and sets the stage for God's arrival.

God spends most of His time taking Job off his self-constructed pedestal; He does not sympathize with Job, nor does He make attempts to pacify him. God immediately takes issue with the claims Job has been spewing concerning God's injustice. Job has been insisting on God's arrival to answer questions and challenges he has prepared. God makes it clear that Job is not in charge of the meeting; God will be asking the questions for Job to answer.

> *Job 38:1-3 Then the Lord answered Job out of the whirlwind: "Who is this that darkens counsel by words without knowledge? Gird up your loins like a man, I will question you, and you shall declare to me."* NRS

Elihu had asked similar questions, but it must have been a sobering moment to hear God asking questions for which Job has no answer. In the passage below, God questions Job concerning his knowledge of creation. By faith we understand that God created the heavens and the earth, but who was there to record the event and explain how everything took place. Imagine Job's mouth being wide open as God challenges him.

157

Job 38:4-7 "Where were you when I laid the foundation of the earth? Tell Me, if you have understanding. Who set its measurements? Since you know, who stretched the line on it? On what were its bases sunk? Or who laid its cornerstone, when the morning stars sang together and all the sons of God shouted for joy?" NASU

God asks the questions, but Job gives no answer. Job has spent a great amount of time and effort preparing his complaint, but upon hearing God, he has no response. God continues by asking Job how the ocean was formed and how it knows its boundaries. We know from *Genesis* that God's Spirit moved across the waters as creation was taking place, but who among humanity can explain how all of this happened? God compares the creation of the oceans to the birthing and care of a child. Job remains silent as he listens to the following words:

Job 38:8-11 "And who took charge of the ocean when it gushed forth like a baby from the womb? That was me! I wrapped it in soft clouds, and tucked it in safely at night. Then I made a playpen for it, a strong playpen so it couldn't run loose, and said, 'Stay here, this is your place. Your wild tantrums are confined to this place." TM

Before the creation of the sun, moon, and stars, God speaks light into existence: "Let there be light!" In the following passage God describes the role of light in defeating the evils of darkness. Does Job have the power and ability to order dawn's arrival and to expose and defeat the evils of the world with the light of God?

Job 38:12-15 "Have you ever given orders to the morning, or shown the dawn its place, that it might take the earth by the edges and shake the wicked out of it? The earth takes shape like clay under a seal; its features stand out like those of a garment. The wicked are denied their light, and their upraised arm is broken." TNIV

Remember an earlier dialogue in which Job gave a lesson to his three friends about silver hidden in the depths of the earth. God asks Job how much he really understands about the inner workings of the earth. It is hard enough to examine the surface of the earth and the sea, but God takes Job even deeper with questions to ponder.

> *Job 38:16-18 "Have you ever gone to where the sea begins or walked in the valleys under the sea? Have the gates of death been opened to you? Have you seen the gates of the deep darkness? Do you understand how wide the earth is? Tell me, if you know all these things."* NCV

God earlier challenged Job concerning his knowledge about creation and light. He has more questions for Job about light and darkness, and he challenges Job on the basis of his length of time on the planet. God is eternal and had no beginning; if Job had been present at creation, he must be tremendously old. In the following statement, God speaks tongue-in-cheek about Job's age to illustrate that Job's knowledge of the earth and its workings is lacking because he was not around during creation.

> *Job 38:19-21 "What is the way to the abode of light? And where does darkness reside? Can you take them to their places? Do you know the paths to their dwellings? Surely you know, for you were already born! You have lived so many years!"* NIV

God sends moisture to refresh and replenish life on earth in the form of snow, rain, or hail, depending on His purposes. Does Job know the answers to the way God works? God presents even more questions as Job and his friends look on and listen in amazement. No one dares attempt to interrupt and present human insights at this point. How would any of us respond if God were to ask us the questions in the verses that follow?

> *Job 38:22-30 "Have you entered the storehouses of the snow, or have you seen the storehouses of the hail, which I have reserved for the time of trouble, for the day of battle and war? What is the way to the place where the light is distributed, or where the east wind is scattered upon the earth? Who has cut a channel for the torrents of rain, and a way for the thunderbolt, to bring rain on a land where no one lives, on the desert, which is empty of human life, to satisfy the waste and desolate land, and to make the ground put forth grass? Has the rain a father, or who has begotten*

the drops of dew? From whose womb did the ice come forth, and who has given birth to the hoarfrost of heaven? The waters become hard like stone, and the face of the deep is frozen." NJB

God's questions about the earth, seas, and sky would be sufficient to convince Job that he knows nothing; however, if that were not enough, the questions about the expanses of the universe completely baffle Job. Are you amazed that constellations were observed, identified, and named in ancient times? How much does Job know about star gazing and how much can he control?

> *Job 38:31-33 "Can you bind the chains of the Pleiades, or loose the cords of Orion? Can you lead forth a constellation in its season, and guide the Bear with her satellites? Do you know the ordinances of the heavens, or fix their rule over the earth?"* NASU

In this next sequence of questions, God presents puzzles surrounding earth. He knows Job does not understand the stars, much less how to direct the changing of the seasons.

God has sole control over rain and drought, and He holds the wisdom to control the clouds and the weather. In the verses below, the phrases "wisdom in the mind" and "understanding to the heart" have been translated in many ways. Many believe God is saying nature can detect weather patterns better than mankind. Plants and animals respond before the weather pattern arrives, but human weather forecasters are often caught by surprise. God has asked Job about his knowledge of these things and how much he can control.

> *Job 38:34-38 "Can you lift up your voice to the clouds, that an abundance of water may cover you? Can you send out lightnings, that they may go, and say to you, 'Here we are'? Who has put wisdom in the mind? Or who has given understanding to the heart? Who can number the clouds by wisdom? Or who can pour out the bottles of heaven, when the dust hardens in clumps, and the clods cling together?"* NKJV

God's questions shift to new challenges of Job's knowledge concerning the creatures of the earth. The next thirty-three verses detail questions about

God's nature and the animals He has made. Job didn't create these creatures, and he does not know how each unique animal is equipped to survive the wild. God's questions make Job's lack of knowledge and power rather evident.

> *Job 38:39-41 "Do you hunt food for the female lion to satisfy the hunger of the young lions while they lie in their dens or hide in the bushes waiting to attack? Who gives food to the birds when their young cry out to God and wander about without food?"* NCV

People observe wild-life, but how much is truly known about the existence of these unique animals? The entirety of *Job 39* is dedicated to questions that neither Job nor his friends can address. How much does Job know about mountain goats?

> *Job 39:1-4 "Do you know when the mountain goats give birth? Do you watch when the doe bears her fawn? Do you count the months till they bear? Do you know the time they give birth? They crouch down and bring forth their young; their labor pains are ended. Their young thrive and grow strong in the wilds; they leave and do not return."* NIV

It appears Job knows precious little about mountain goats because he has nothing to say. Job's comments before God's arrival indicated he wanted to be on equal footing with the Almighty, but he is quickly learning that his knowledge is far below that of the Creator. What kind of knowledge does he have about wild donkeys?

> *Job 39:5-8 "Who has let the wild donkey go free? Who has loosed the bonds of the swift donkey to whom I have given the arid plain for his home and the salt land for his dwelling place? He scorns the tumult of the city; he hears not the shouts of the driver. He ranges the mountains as his pasture, and he searches after every green thing."* ESV

Remember that God's questions are directed at Job to convince and humble the man concerning his knowledge of all things belonging to God. Neither Job nor his friends have a clue as to how creation took place and how animals in the wild make it without human intervention. Job hasn't responded through the barrage of questions, and he will continue to be silent as God next asks about the wild ox.

> *Job 39:9-12 "Will the wild ox agree to serve you and stay by your feeding box at night? Can you hold it to the plowed row with a harness so it will plow the valleys for you? Will you depend on the wild ox for its great strength and leave your heavy work for it to do? Can you trust the ox to bring in your grain and gather it to your threshing floor?"* NCV

The animals being described exist in the wild without any help from humans. God continues by asking Job about the nature of ostriches. How do baby ostriches make it through to adult status when their mothers have no concern? The ostrich has amazing abilities surpassing those of a horse controlled by a rider.

> *Job 39:13-18 "The ostriches' wings flap joyously with the pinion and plumage of love, for she abandons her eggs to the earth and warms them in the dust, and she forgets that a foot may crush them, or that a wild beast may trample them. She treats her young cruelly, as if they were not hers; though her labor be in vain, she is unconcerned because God has made her forget wisdom and has not given her a share of understanding. When she lifts herself on high, she laughs at the horse and his rider."* NASU

After God compares the abilities of an ostrich to those of a horse, He has questions for Job concerning horses. Is Job the one who equipped horses with their tremendous strength and abilities to assist mankind on the battlefield? Job was not present when horses were created, and he certainly doesn't understand where their strength originates.

> *Job 39:19-25 "Do you give the horse its strength or clothe its neck with a flowing mane? Do you make it leap like a locust striking terror with its proud snorting? It paws fiercely, rejoicing in its strength, and charges into the fray. It laughs at fear, afraid of nothing; it does not shy away from the sword. The quiver rattles against its side, along with the flashing spear and lance. In frenzied excitement it eats up the ground; it cannot stand still when the trumpet*

162

sounds. At the blast of the trumpet it snorts, 'Aha!' It catches the scent of battle from afar, the shout of commanders and the battle cry." TNIV

God ends His questions about the animal world by asking Job about his human ability to control hawks and eagles. Was it Job who blessed these amazing creatures with their abilities? God describes the habitats and behaviors of these amazing birds.

Job 39:26-30 "Is it by your wisdom that the hawk soars, and spreads its wings toward the south? Is it at your command that the eagle mounts up and makes its nest on high? It lives on the rock and makes its home in the fastness of the rocky crag. From there it spies the prey; its eyes see it from far away. Its young ones suck up blood; and where the slain are, there it is." NRS

After hearing this barrage of questions about God's nature and creatures, it is no wonder that Job and his friends have remained silent. Job has been demanding that his righteousness proves God is wrong in allowing him to suffer. However, God has proven beyond doubt that Job knows nothing about the nature of His decisions and that Job has no creative ability. It appears that God has kept an open invitation for Job to respond, but on the following question, God demands an answer.

Job 40:1-2 The Lord said to Job: "Will the one who contends with the Almighty correct him? Let him who accuses God answer him!" NIV

God has put Job on the spot to respond, but his tone of voice changes from earlier dialogues. As the passage below is read, the reader is able to detect sounds of remorse and humility.

Job 40:3-5 Then Job replied to the Lord, "I am nothing— how could I ever find the answers? I will cover my mouth with my hand. I have said too much already. I have nothing more to say." NLT

This was a good start, but God has more to say concerning Job's denigrating comments, fueled by his arrogance. Can you hear the thunder of God's voice in the following verses?

Job 40:6-9   Then the Lord answered Job out of the whirlwind, and said: "Now prepare yourself like a man; I will question you, and you shall answer Me: Would you indeed annul My judgment? Would you condemn Me that you may be justified? Have you an arm like God? Or can you thunder with a voice like His? NKJV

Job's problem has been his pompous pride, and this point is crystal clear in the following verses. Job has previously identified people who exceed him in wickedness, and he has voiced his displeasure that they go unpunished. However, he can find no one who exceeds him in arrogance. God groups the arrogant and the wicked together and tells Job to reprimand and humble them. If Job can do this, God will admit that Job can save himself. In essence God has said, "In my love and wisdom, I delivered pain to you to save your soul from the arrogant pit you have been digging." Since Job has tried to place himself on the same level with God, God challenges Job to find a way to humble the proud. If Job can accomplish this, God says He is willing to concede that Job has the power to save himself.

Job 40:10-14   "Adorn yourself with eminence and dignity, and clothe yourself with honor and majesty. Pour out the overflowings of your anger, and look on everyone who is proud, and make him low. Look on everyone who is proud, and humble him, and tread down the wicked where they stand. Hide them in the dust together; bind them in the hidden place. Then I will also confess to you, that your own right hand can save you." NASU

This next sequence of verses has long puzzled translators and Bible scholars. Which animal is being described below: whale, hippopotamus, elephant, or none of the above? Most have settled on the hippopotamus because of the size and the description of its lying under the lotus plants. It appears the creature is amphibious, which would also describe the hippopotamus.

Rather than wrestle over the species, I suggest seeking a deeper message. Notice that God compares the creation of Behemoth to the creation of mankind. He goes on to describe the strength of Behemoth and the life of leisure it leads. A real key is found when God says, "He is the first of the ways of God." This really draws a link between Behemoth and human

164

beings. One of the best explanations I have considered hypothesizes that Behemoth symbolizes mankind in general. Only his Maker can approach the animal with a sword; this is comparable to humans being controllable only by their Creator. Job has been living the life of Behemoth, a life so filled with plenty that he had come to believe he was king of the universe.

> *Job 40:15-24   "Behold now, Behemoth, which I made as well as you; he eats grass like an ox. Behold now, his strength in his loins, and his power in the muscles of his belly. He bends his tail like a cedar; the sinews of his thighs are knit together. His bones are tubes of bronze; his limbs are like bars of iron. He is the first of the ways of God; let his maker bring near his sword. Surely the mountains bring him food, and all the beasts of the field play there. Under the lotus plants he lies down, in the covert of the reeds and the marsh. The lotus plants cover him with shade; the willows of the brook surround him. If a river rages, he is not alarmed; he is confident, though the Jordan rushes to his mouth. Can anyone capture him when he is on watch, with barbs can anyone pierce his nose?"* NAS

Another puzzling creature is described in great length in *Job 41*; Leviathan has created as much head scratching as Behemoth. On the literal level, it appears Leviathan is an alligator, but symbolically it appears Leviathan is Satan. The comparisons will be made as *Job 41* is examined in short segments. An alligator cannot be caught with a fish-hook, and who would want to attempt holding down his tongue? An alligator cannot communicate on the human level, so the latter part of the following verses seems to point to Satan's communication tactics. It would be foolish to accept a bargain from Satan, regardless of how appealing the deal might sound. Neither Satan nor an alligator will serve the one who decides to play with them. Bargaining with Satan is equal to selling one's soul to the devil. Once again, Job has played the role of Behemoth and had fallen into the grips of Leviathan, the devil!

> *Job 41:1-4 "Leviathan, too! Can you catch him with a fish-hook or hold his tongue down with a rope? Can you put a cane through his nostrils or pierce his jaw with a hook? Will he plead lengthily with you, addressing you in diffident*

As the description continues, one can easily see references describing an alligator.   Anyone battling with an alligator will never forget the confrontation. On the other hand, what about a wrestling match with Satan? The suffering of Job should certainly convince readers that Satan's bite is worse than that of alligator. How interesting that Satan seems to disappear after chapter two of the book of *Job*, but God could be refreshing Job's mind about his encounters in the "alligator pond," leading to his loss of health and wealth.

> *Job 41:5-9 "Will you play with him as with a bird? Or will
> you bind him for your maidens? Will the traders bargain
> over him? Will they divide him among the merchants? Can
> you fill his skin with harpoons, or his head with fishing
> spears? Lay your hand on him; remember the battle; you
> will not do it again! Behold, your expectation is false; will
> you be laid low even at the sight of him?"* NAS

The passage below ends with an interesting parallel, applicable to both alligators and Satan; obviously, both are created beings that one should avoid. If no man can win a hand-to-hand battle with alligators or with Satan, does Job really think he can win a confrontation with the God who created both? God owes no man anything; all of creation belongs to the Almighty.

> *Job 41:10-11 "No one is so fierce that he dares to arouse
> him; who then is he that can stand before Me? Who has
> given to Me that I should repay him? Whatever is under the
> whole heaven is Mine."* NAS

In analyzing Leviathan, I have viewed many pictures of alligators, and the description surely does fit. When one sees their armored, lizard-like bodies, muscular tails, and powerful jaws, it is clear warning to avoid contact.   The Creator of the alligator furnishes Job with the following description:

> *Job 41:12-17 "I will not conceal his limbs, his mighty
> power, or his graceful proportions. Who can remove his
> outer coat? Who can approach him with a double bridle?
> Who can open the doors of his face, with his terrible teeth all*

around? His rows of scales are his pride, shut up tightly as
with a seal; one is so near another that no air can come
between them. They are joined one to another; they stick
together and cannot be parted." NKJV

The next part of the description could be considered hyperbole, a figure
of speech exaggerating the alligator's ferocity, but it also sounds like be a
picture of hell fire connected with Satan's domain.

Job 41:18-21 "When it snorts, flashes of light are thrown
out, and its eyes look like the light at dawn. Flames blaze
from its mouth; sparks of fire shoot out. Smoke pours out
of its nose, as if coming from a large pot over a hot fire.
Its breath sets coals on fire, and flames come out of its
mouth." NCV

God describes Leviathan as a creature to be feared! This is certainly
true concerning both an alligator and Satan. As the description below
expands, Leviathan is pictured as impervious to man's attempts to injure or
destroy. While this could also be considered as hyperbole concerning the
alligator, it more likely pictures mankind's inability to battle successfully
with Satan. Only God has the power to confront the evil one; Satan laughs at
human efforts to overcome his weapons of destruction.

Job 41:22-29 "In his neck abides strength, and terror
dances before him. The folds of his flesh stick together,
firmly cast on him and immovable. His heart is hard as a
stone, hard as the lower millstone. When he raises himself
up the mighty are afraid; at the crashing they are beside
themselves. Though the sword reaches him, it does not
avail, nor the spear, the dart, or the javelin. He counts
iron as straw, and bronze as rotten wood. The arrow
cannot make him flee; for him sling stones are turned to
stubble. Clubs are counted as stubble; he laughs at the
rattle of javelins." ESV

Both alligators and Satan stir the waters, leaving a path of destruction
behind them. When God concludes His description of Leviathan, it becomes
absolutely clear that God's issue with Job is over pride and that Leviathan
symbolizes Satan, ruler of all who are arrogant. Elihu, in his mediator role,

167

had pointed to Job's narcissism as the reason for his suffering; God puts the stamp on it. The human race is much like Behemoth, and Satan is similar to Leviathan. Job has had his meeting with Leviathan when God sent Satan to put Job to the test.

> *Job 41:30-34 "His undersides are jagged potsherds, leaving a trail in the mud like a threshing sledge. He makes the depths churn like a boiling caldron and stirs up the sea like a pot of ointment. Behind him he leaves a glistening wake; one would think the deep had white hair. Nothing on earth is his equal — a creature without fear. He looks down on all that are haughty; he is king over all that are proud."* NIV

How will Job respond to God's message? Will God's efforts work in bringing Job to his knees? Having listened to the voice of God, Job's encounter has caused him to realize his lack of knowledge about the Almighty. Job recants everything said earlier.

> *Job 42:1-6 Then Job replied to the Lord: "I know that you can do anything, and no one can stop you. You asked, 'Who is this that questions my wisdom with such ignorance?' It is I—and I was talking about things I knew nothing about, things far too wonderful for me. You said, 'Listen and I will speak! I have some questions for you, and you must answer them.' I had only heard about you before, but now I have seen you with my own eyes. I take back everything I said, and I sit in dust and ashes to show my repentance."* NLT

Job responds wisely by humbling himself in the presence of the Almighty; however, the friends remain standing there in silence. When God says Job has spoken of Him correctly, that is not a reference to Job's dialogue found in twenty-eight chapters from *Job 3-31*; it acknowledges Job's confession. When Job apologizes for his previous claims and retracts his inaccurate comments, he is the only one of the four who does so. The three friends have had much to say during that same section of the book of *Job*; however, they say nothing to acknowledge God's power. One of my friends used to say, "Do you have lock-jaw?" God calls on Eliphaz, Bildad, and Zophar to offer sacrifices for themselves while Job prays for them, and the three friends follow through. When God forgives, He forgives completely to remember no more.

Job 42:7-9 When Yahweh had finished saying this to Job, he said to Eliphaz of Teman, "I burn with anger against you and your two friends, for not having spoken correctly about me as my servant Job has done. So now find seven bullocks and seven rams, and take them back with you to my servant Job and make a burnt offering for yourselves, while Job, my servant, offers prayers for you. I shall show him favor and shall not inflict my displeasure on you for not having spoken about me correctly, as my servant Job has done." Eliphaz of Teman, Bildad of Shuah and Zophar of Naamath went away to do as Yahweh had ordered, and Yahweh listened to Job with favor. NJB

Once again a reminder that God had absolutely nothing to say in the way of correcting or instructing Elihu; this silence speaks volumes! Job may not have been patient through his suffering, but he certainly did persevere; furthermore, he helped his friends through prayer to receive God's forgiveness. Job is a wonderful study of how to respond to disasters that come in life. Believing that the book of *Job* tells a salvation story, the final chapter of this volume will illustrate that the second half of Job's life is symbolic of eternal blessings.

STUDY GUIDE – Chapter 12

1. After demanding audience with God, why is Job silent when God arrives?

2. Why does God ask Job about his age?

3. Explain how animals and natural surrounding can predict weather changes.

4. Describe Job's demeanor when he responds to God in *Job 40:3-5.*

5. What is significant about God's description of Behemoth?

6. What is significant about God's description of Leviathan?

7. What does Job have to say in his last recorded comments in *Job 42:1-6?*

8. Why does God not correct Elihu in His closing comments?

CHAPTER 13

– I'VE NEVER HAD IT SO GOOD!

The story of salvation in the book of Job

The suffering and redemption of Job serve as a message of salvation for this modern age. Job is described as a man who had it all—extreme wealth, good health, and a large family. After God sends Satan to test Job, he is left void of possessions, family, and personal health. What a swing in circumstances! Some have described such changes as moving from the penthouse to the outhouse. This chapter will apply the story of Job's struggle to this current age by illustrating that when in good times, it is important to be humble in realizing that God provides. When suffering, one should humble self to the point of seeking God's grace and mercy. The apostle Paul claimed to have the secret to these extreme conditions of life.

> *Philippians 4:11-13 I have learned to be content whatever the circumstances. I know what it is to be in need, and I know what it is to have plenty. I have learned the secret of being content in any and every situation, whether well fed or hungry, whether living in plenty or in want. I can do everything through him who gives me strength.* NIV

How do we gain this strength from God? In another letter, Paul reveals the method for connecting with God. We must find a way to have daily communication with God through prayer, and we must find reasons to be thankful in every situation that comes our way. Paul's formula is as follows:

> *1 Thessalonians 5:16-18 Rejoice always, pray continually, give thanks in all circumstances; for this is God's will for you in Christ Jesus.* TNIV

Paul's words in these two passages describe a relationship with God that comes with salvation. When Job was on earth, these verses had not been

171

written, but the principle was as true then as it is today. God has always had provisions for establishing a relationship with those who seek Him and express their thanks. It took Job some time to arrive, but how was he able to persevere to the point of salvation? The answer to this question has everything to do with our salvation today.

For about two decades after the church began on Pentecost in 30 AD, Christians were so busy finding converts and encouraging each other that no effort was made to develop a New Testament. When the church began to struggle over doctrinal issues, the apostle Paul wrote thirteen letters that were later included in the New Testament at the beginning of the fifth century. Before Christians began to write, and before twenty-seven books were canonized into the Bible, what was used as evidence that Jesus was the Christ? The only written work available in the earliest days of Christianity was the Old Testament, in which principles of righteousness and prophecies about Jesus could be found and taught.

The book of *Acts* tells about additional converts after Pentecost; one of the most interesting occurs when a eunuch from Ethiopia was returning to his home country after a visit to Jerusalem. The man was reading from *Isaiah* while riding in a chariot. The Spirit of God guided the evangelist Philip to a meeting with the Ethiopian eunuch, who invited him to join him in the chariot. The eunuch was reading a scroll from what we know today as *Isaiah 53*, a prophecy about Jesus' trial and crucifixion. Philip used this Old Testament document to teach the salvation message, and the eunuch responded.

> *Acts 8:34-39 The eunuch asked Philip, "About whom, may I ask you, does the prophet say this, about himself or about someone else?" Then Philip began to speak, and starting with this scripture, he proclaimed to him the good news about Jesus. As they were going along the road, they came to some water; and the eunuch said, "Look, here is water! What is to prevent me from being baptized?" And Philip said, "If you believe with all your heart, you may." And he replied, "I believe that Jesus Christ is the Son of God." He commanded the chariot to stop, and both of them, Philip and the eunuch, went down into the water, and Philip baptized him. When they came up out of the water, the Spirit of the*

Lord snatched Philip away; the eunuch saw him no more,
and went on his way rejoicing. NRS

If the eunuch had been reading from the book of *Job*, God's message of salvation could also have been taught effectively. In understanding how *Job* relates the story of salvation, notice Job's progression through suffering, to finally submitting to God's perfect will and to his receiving boundless blessings.

MANKIND IS IN NEED OF RELATIONSHIP WITH GOD

When all is going well, it is tempting to take great pride in concluding that human effort accomplished all and to overlook the true source of blessings. Pride takes a great toll when temptation has its way; the urge to elevate self is often coupled with demeaning others who are considered less deserving. Even more disastrous is the tendency to forget God in the process. However, God sends blessings to encourage recipients to revere Him and serve others in His name.

> *James 1:17-18 Whatever is good and perfect comes down to us from God our Father, who created all the lights in the heavens. He never changes or casts a shifting shadow. He chose to give birth to us by giving us his true word. And we, out of all creation, became his prized possession.* NLT

Because humanity is His prized possession, God sends all kinds of blessings, but how do we respond to God's gifts? When reading Job's comments prior to his encounter with God, it becomes clear that Job believed his own goodness had gained his status. The tendency to follow Job's pattern of pride over prosperous times drives many to overlook the message above and sink into attempts at self-sufficiency.

There is nothing evil about money or having possessions; furthermore, money is not the root of all evil as some persons claim. The covetous person says, "I'm not greedy; I just want all the land that touches mine." The problem stems from the "love of money" and the desire to have more.

> *1 Timothy 6:10 For the love of money is a root of all sorts of evil, and some by longing for it have wandered away from the faith and pierced themselves with many griefs.* NAS

Jesus presented a deep message about the dangers involved with loving money when he told about a poor man named Lazarus and a man who had great riches; the great reversal took place after death with Lazarus being blessed and the rich man suffering torment. He also told about a rich young man whose wealth came before his desire to follow God. After his conversation with the young man, Jesus had the following to say to His followers:

> *Matthew 19:23-24 "I tell you the truth, it is hard for a rich man to enter the kingdom of heaven. Again I tell you, it is easier for a camel to go through the eye of a needle than for a rich man to enter the kingdom of God."* NIV

It is easy to rejoice and bask in the sunshine of blessings, but what about finding peace and contentment when the world is upside down? Remember that the apostle Paul claimed to have the secret for contentment in times of plenty or in times of want—God provides! Job took great pleasure during his days of prosperity, and when losses came his way, his immediate response seems to be one of acceptance.

> *Job 2:10 He replied, "You are talking like a foolish woman. Shall we accept good from God, and not trouble?" In all this, Job did not sin in what he said.* TM

After sitting in silence and misery for seven days, Job breaks the silence, condemning God for his condition. When tallying all of Job's losses, one can understand why Job was not having a party to rejoice. How can one truly rejoice in all circumstances when some situations are virtually unbearable? As difficult as it may be, Paul claimed in *1 Thessalonians 5:16-18* that we should give thanks in all circumstances; this may come with great difficulty while going through a struggle.

Job's mouth uttered truth in the above verse, but his heart and brain were not working together. In his next nine speeches, Job does not humble himself, nor does he seek God's mercy. Rather than giving thanks for his circumstances, he condemns and criticizes the Almighty, accusing God of injustice. We do not have control over the circumstances of life that come our way, but we do have control over our responses to the circumstances.

If the reader still has doubts about reasons for giving thanks in all circumstances, it may be time to re-read chapter two of this volume to help recall blessings through suffering. True friendships are not developed when all is going well; valuable growth in relationships takes place in difficult times. The same is true with man's relationship with God; friendship with God can be strengthened through suffering.

NECESSITY OF A MEDIATOR

Job finally learned the lesson, but it didn't appear that he would ever humble himself and learn through his suffering. However, about the time it appeared Job had hit the end of the rope, Elihu had something to say. Job's mind was still in a fog; rather than asking God for a mediator to help him know what to do, he sought a mediator to correct God.

> *Job 9:33-34 "If only there were someone to arbitrate between us, to lay his hand upon us both, someone to remove God's rod from me, so that his terror would frighten me no more."* NIV

At least give Job credit for realizing he was incapable of confronting God without some kind of intervention. The salvation story today is the same; we also must realize our human limits and seek Jesus' intervention in coming to know God. We need the Mediator Jesus Christ! This great truth is presented in the following passage:

> *Romans 23:22-25 God makes people right with himself through their faith in Jesus Christ. This is true for all who believe in Christ, because all people are the same; everyone has sinned and fallen short of God's glorious standard, and all need to be made right with God by his grace, which is a free gift. They need to be made free from sin through Jesus Christ. God sent him to die in our place to take away our sins. We receive forgiveness through faith in the blood of Jesus' death. This showed that God always does what is right and fair, as in the past when he was patient and did not punish people for their sins.* NCV

LISTENING TO THE MEDIATOR

Elihu was the answer to Job's prayer for intercession. Because he has information straight from God's throne, Elihu's nature could have been rather frightening to Job. To alleviate this possibility, Elihu tells Job, "I'm made of clay just as you are." This statement would have been absolutely unnecessary under normal circumstances, but Elihu's complete message will prove the need for Elihu's statement.

> *Job 33:6-7 "Truly I am as your spokesman before God; I also have been formed out of clay. Surely no fear of me will terrify you, nor will my hand be heavy on you."* NKJV

In *Job 33* and *Job 36*, Elihu has much to say about his spirit filled mission from God. While he stood as God's spokesperson to Job, he further claims his mission was to speak in God's behalf. God had endowed Elihu with knowledge from the Throne, knowledge that Eliphaz, Bildad, and Zophar did not possess. Acknowledging that his information did not come from his own intellect and insight, he says his message would come from afar. Furthermore, because God was inspiring him to speak, he claimed to be speaking absolute truth because he had been given perfect knowledge.

God sent Jesus as our Mediator, and scripture presents evidence of Jesus' mediation through statements that parallel Elihu's mission.

1. Human Nature

> ➤ **Elihu**
>
> *Job 33:6 "I also have been formed out of clay."* NKJV
>
> ➤ **Jesus**
>
> *John 18:39 "For this reason I was born, and for this I came into the world."* NIV
>
> *John 1:1 In the beginning was the Word, and the Word was with God, and the Word was God.* NIV
>
> *John 1:14 The Word became flesh and made his dwelling among us.* NIV

2. Speaking from Inspiration

> ➢ **Elihu**

Job 36:3 "I will get my knowledge from afar." WEB

> ➢ **Jesus**

John 12:49 "I did not speak on my own, but the Father who sent me commanded me to say all that I have spoken." TNIV

3. Speaking in God's Behalf

> ➢ **Elihu**

Job 36:2 "Wait for me a little, and I will show you that there is yet more to be said in God's behalf." NASU

> ➢ **Jesus**

John 12:50 "I know that his command leads to eternal life. So whatever I say is just what the Father has told me to say." TNIV

4. Presenting Absolute Truth

> ➢ **Elihu**

Job 36:4 "For truly my words are not false; one who is perfect in knowledge is with you." NRS

> ➢ **Jesus**

In the Gospels, Jesus said, "I tell you the truth," seventy-six times. No wonder He could say, "I am the way and the truth and the life." John 14:6 NIV

Job knew there was something special about Elihu; consequently, he says nothing in response to Elihu's message. It was imperative for him to hear the things Elihu had to say. Elihu prepared Job for God's arrival by giving him a preview of God's message to follow, telling Job his arrogance was standing in the way of a proper relationship with God. This is the exact message God delivered to Job through a barrage of questions that revealed Job's human inabilities and his misconceptions about God's creation and God's ways.

Just as Elihu led Job into the presence of the Lord, Jesus does the same for us today. Therefore, it is imperative that we listen to the Gospel message of Jesus to receive the salvation God has planned for those who accept His Son. Concerning His role as Mediator, consider these words spoken by Jesus:

> *John 14:6-7 "I am the way, the truth, and the life. No one can come to the Father except through me. If you had really known me, you would know who my Father is. From now on, you do know him and have seen him!"* NLT

RESPONDING IN HUMILITY

Because Job had listened to Elihu's mediation, the message of God could be heard plainly—the message: Job is not God! Job's problem was arrogance, but after paying attention to Elihu, he was able to experience God and to humble himself before his Maker.

No man can reach God through human effort. Jesus Christ proved the point more fully when He came to earth in human form and humbled himself to die on a cross. Jesus said He could have called twelve legions of angels to save Him, but rather than summoning sixty-thousand angels, He submitted to the whip, to the crown of thorns, to ridicule, and to death on the cross.

> *Philippians 2:5-8 In your lives you must think and act like Christ Jesus. Christ himself was like God in everything. But he did not think that being equal with God was something to be used for his own benefit. But he gave up his place with God and made himself nothing. He was born as a man and became like a servant. And when he was living as a man, he humbled himself and was fully obedient to God, even when that caused his death—death on a cross.* NCV

Imagine the shock of Jesus' followers, when their Lord and Master had them remove their sandals so He could wash their feet. Simon Peter at first refused the offer, but when Jesus said he would have no part in His kingdom without being washed by the Master, he submitted. What an act of humility when Jesus knelt to wash feet!

Perhaps we should not be amazed when we realize that Jesus began His ministry on earth with one of the most humble actions one can imagine. Can you imagine John's amazement and shock when Jesus the Christ, the One John was promoting, came to the Jordan and asked John to baptize Him.

> *Matthew 3:13-15 Then Jesus came from Galilee to the Jordan to be baptized by John. But John tried to deter him, saying, "I need to be baptized by you, and do you come to me?" Jesus replied, "Let it be so now; it is proper for us to do this to fulfill all righteousness." Then John consented.* NIV

The most logical and reasonable explanation for why Jesus was baptized is that He was showing His followers the way to humble themselves. What surrounded the baptism of Jesus to help us accept this premise?

1) The Spirit of God descended on Jesus – *Matthew 3:16*
   Salvation brings the gift of the Holy Spirit– *Acts 2:38*
2) Jesus' baptism confirmed that He was God's Son – *Matthew 3:17*
   We are born again to become sons of God – *John 3:5-6; Galatians 4:4-7*
3) Jesus' baptism prepared him to withstand Satan – *Matthew 4:1*
   New life prepares Christians to overcome evil – *Romans 6:1-7; 1 John 1:7*
4) Jesus was baptized to fulfill all righteousness
   (do what is right) *Matthew3:15*
   Believers comply for conscience sake in doing what is right – *1 Peter 3:21*

Jesus leads His followers into the presence of God through knowledge of His example as role model, his teaching, and his suffering. To prove without doubt that our response to His suffering is vital in the salvation story, consider the suffering of Jesus Christ.

> *Hebrews 2:8-11 For in putting all things under him he made no exceptions. At present, it is true, we are not able to see that all things are under him, but we do see Jesus, who was for a short while made less than the angels, now crowned with glory and honor because he submitted to death; so that by God's grace his experience of death should benefit all*

179

humanity.   It was fitting that God, for whom and through whom everything exists, should, in bringing many sons to glory, make perfect through suffering the leader of their salvation.   For consecrator and consecrated are all of the same stock; that is why he is not ashamed to call them brothers. NJB

Because Jesus showed the way to salvation through His suffering, who am I to think that I should escape suffering? Fox's Book of Martyrs tells of many followers of Christ who went to their death praising the Lord for the opportunity to share in the sufferings of Jesus Christ. Jesus' prayer in the Garden of Gethsemane was to "let this cup pass from me." Looking death in the face was not pleasant; however, Jesus added to the prayer, "But Your will be done." Jesus was made perfect through His suffering, and we are blessed in our suffering if we submit to God and seek His will to be done in our lives.

SALVATION BRINGS ETERNAL BLESSINGS

The message of the book of *Job* is one of salvation, a story early Christians could relate to potential converts as they explained that humans need a relationship with their Creator. The book of *Job* contains the same message today for those willing to submit themselves to the Almighty. No two journeys are exactly alike in timing, intensity, and methods, but there are some general commonalities in the journey to salvation.

- All humans experience life's peaks and valleys.
- Some rely on human effort to resolve their struggles.
- Others realize their personal weaknesses and limitations.
- Those on the right track experience the Mediator Jesus.
- They humble themselves to follow Jesus and to be born again.
- In this new life they grow in relationship with God.
- Their physical death brings full reality of relationship with God.

The Narrator tells of Job's blessings after his steps to humble himself before God. The significance of God's gifts to Job symbolizes what God has in store eternally for others who follow Job's path of perseverance. In order to receive these blessings, Job humbled himself to the point of loving those who had been so condemning of him.

Job 42:10-11 And the Lord restored the fortunes of Job, when he had prayed for his friends. And the Lord gave Job twice as much as he had before. Then came to him all his brothers and sisters and all who had known him before, and ate bread with him in his house. And they showed him sympathy and comforted him for all the evil that the Lord had brought upon him. And each of them gave him a piece of money and a ring of gold. ESV

When one is born physically, the person receives a body that dies; when one is born spiritually, the person receives a spiritual body that will never die. This spiritual body is the body that is eternal. God's followers are given eternal life while physically alive, but the full reality does not take place until this physical life ends.

John 11:25-26 Jesus said to her, "I am the resurrection and the life. He who believes in Me, though he may die, he shall live. And whoever lives and believes in Me shall never die. Do you believe this?" NKJV

New Testament writers give glimpses of the eternal blessings that await those who meet the Mediator and respond to God as Job had done. When Jesus was tested by a teacher of the law about the greatest of the commandments, He did not list even one of the Ten Commandments. All of the rules and commandments of God are summed up in two overriding principles.

Matthew 22:37-40 Jesus replied: "'Love the Lord your God with all your heart and with all your soul and with all your mind.' This is the first and greatest commandment. And the second is like it: 'Love your neighbor as yourself.' All the Law and the Prophets hang on these two commandments." TNIV

Eliphaz, Bildad, and Zophar had made many accusations concerning Job, but after listening to God's message, it was time for Job to forgive his misdirected friends and others who had condemned and ridiculed him. When Jesus was on earth, He urged His followers to forgive those who are abusive.

Luke 6:27-31 "But I say to you who hear: Love your enemies, do good to those who hate you, bless those who

curse you, and pray for those who spitefully use you. To him who strikes you on the one cheek, offer the other also. And from him who takes away your cloak, do not withhold your tunic either. Give to everyone who asks of you. And from him who takes away your goods do not ask them back. And just as you want men to do to you, you also do to them likewise. NKJV

After Job fell to his knees in humble submission to God and after he had humbled himself before his friends by forgiving and praying for them, the Lord not only blessed Job with riches, He also blessed Job's new family.

Job 42:12-15 The Lord blessed the last part of Job's life even more than he had blessed the first. Job owned fourteen thousand sheep, six thousand camels, two thousand head of cattle, and one thousand donkeys. He was the father of seven sons and three daughters. He called the oldest daughter Jemimah, the second Keziah, and the youngest Keren Happuch. There were no other women in the whole world as beautiful as Job's daughters. Their father gave them a share of the inheritance along with their brothers. GNT

The names of Job's daughters indicate beauty. When translated from Hebrew, the name Jemimah means dove, Keziah refers to cassia, a variety of cinnamon used as a perfume, and Keren Happuch is a small box used for eye make-up. What about the deeper meaning of Job's children? It is possible that his family symbolizes all who follow in Job's steps, as heirs of the lessons he learned. God's followers are precious and beautiful in His sight.

Great blessings come to those who follow the words of Jesus. John recorded Jesus' explanation to His followers that better circumstances were awaiting them after their physical lives end. Salvation results in a heavenly home that far surpasses earthly dwellings.

John 14:2-3 "In my Father's house are many mansions; if it were not so, I would have told you; for I go to prepare a place for you. And if I go and prepare a place for you, I come again, and will receive you unto myself; that where I am, (there) ye may be also." ASV

On this side of death, everyone is subjected to pain, suffering, and losses of every type; however, eternal salvation brings a reversal of circumstances that make perseverance through suffering worth the effort.

> *Revelation 21:3-4 And I heard a loud voice from the throne saying, "Look! God's dwelling place is now among the people, and he will dwell with them. They will be his people, and God himself will be with them and be their God. 'He will wipe every tear from their eyes. There will be no more death' or mourning or crying or pain. For the old order of things has passed away." TNIV*

The Narrator ends the story of Job by telling readers that Job's second part of life was blessed for 140 years. The number 14 is double the number 7, a perfect number often symbolizing forgiveness and perfection in the Bible, and the number 10 symbolizes totality. Job's age in his second life is symbolized by forgiveness, times totality, doubled. What a picture of eternal salvation for those who follow Job's example!

> *Job 42:16-17 After this, Job lived a hundred and forty years; he saw his children and their children to the fourth generation. And so he died, old and full of years. NIV*

Just as Job was double blessed in the second part of his life, Christians will also be blessed in the second part of their lives. Once one views the book of *Job* in the light of everyday relevance for this generation, acceptance of suffering is much more likely. The message of *Job* encourages each of us to deal with personal losses and health issues by following Job's example of perseverance, reliance on God, and forgiveness of others. Hopefully, this volume will help readers understand that great rewards await those who are trained by seeking God's mercy to alleviate their suffering.

STUDY GUIDE – Chapter 13

1. How was the salvation story presented before the New Testament was written and canonized?

2. What is the source for all blessings?

3. Explain why pride stands in the way of salvation.

4. Compare Elihu and Jesus as mediators.

5. How important is Jesus as our mediator today?

6. Since Jesus was God in the flesh, why did He humble Himself?

7. In what ways can we humble ourselves upon learning about our mediator?

8. How does the "second part" of Job's life symbolize eternal life?

Bibliography

Andersen, Francis I. *Job*. Tyndale Old Testament Commentaries. Downers Grove, Illinois: InterVarsity, 1976

Clarke, Adam, Commentary and Critical Notes, Vol III, The Methodist Book Concern, New York, Cincinnati, Chicago, 1826

Ewert, David, From Ancient Tablets to Modern Translations, Grand Rapids, Michigan: Zondervan Corporation, 1983

Fox, John, Fox's Book of Martyrs, (edited by William Byran Forbush) Universal Book and Bible House, Philadelphia, Pa., 1926

Garrett, Duane L., Job. Shepherd's Notes. Nashville, Tennessee: Holman Reference, 1998

Hobbs, Lottie Beth, Victory Over Trials, Encouragement from the Life of Job, Fort Worth, Texas: Harvest Publications, 1990

Kubler-Ross, Elisabeth, On Death and Dying, New York: Simon & Schuster, Inc., 1997

McKenna, David L., The Communicator's Commentary on Job, Waco, Texas; Word, Inc., 1986

Ogilvie, Lloyd J., The Communicator's Commentary, Job, World Books, Publisher, Waco, Texas, 1986

Van Selms, A, *Job*: *A Practical Commentary*, translated from the Dutch edition *Job: Een praktische bijbelverklaring,* by John Vriend, Grand Rapids Michigan: Eerdmans Publishing, 1985

Bible Versions Utilized:

American Standard Version, Nashville, Tennessee: Thomas Nelson Publishers

Bible in Basic English, Cambridge, Massachusetts: Cambridge University Press, 1965

English Standard Version, Wheaton, Illinois: Crossway Bibles, a division of Good News Publishers, 2001

Good News Translation, New York: HarperCollins Publishers, 1976

King James Version, Nashville, Tennessee: Thomas Nelson Publishers, 1978

Living Bible, Wheaton, Illinois, Coverdale House Publishers, LTD, 1972

New American Standard: La Habra, California, Foundation Press, 1971

New American Standard Updated, Anaheim California,
  Foundation Press, 1995

New Century Version, New York: Thomas Nelson & Sons, 1987

New English Translation, www.netbible.com,
  Biblical Studies Press, LLC, 1996

New Jerusalem Bible. London: Darton, Longman, & Todd, 1985

New International Version. Grand Rapids, Michigan:
  Zondervan Publishers 1985

New King James Version, New York: Thomas Nelson & Sons, 1982

New Living Testament, Carol Stream, Illinois: Tyndale House, 1996

New Revised Standard, New York: HarperCollins, 1989

Revised Standard Version, New York: Thomas Nelson & Sons, 1971

The Message, paraphrase by Eugene H. Peterson, Colorado Springs,
  Colorado: NavPress, 2002

Today's New International Version, Grand Rapids, Michigan:
  Zondervan Publishers, 2002

World English Bible, www.ebible.org/web/

CPSIA information can be obtained at www.ICGtesting.com
Printed in the USA
LVOW01s2222080514

384973LV00020B/398/P